CW00546504

THE ACE CAFE
THEN AND NOW

The Ace was tea . . . chips . . . and speed!
CHARLIE WILLIAMS

THE ACE CAFE
THEN AND NOW

Edited by Winston Ramsey

Credits

ISBN: 1 870067 46 6

Compiled, edited and designed by Winston Ramsey, Editor-in-Chief *After the Battle*

PUBLISHERS
Battle of Britain International Limited
Church House, Church St., London E15 3JA
Telephone (020) 8534 8833

PRINTERS
Printed in Great Britain by Heronsgate Ltd, Basildon, Essex.

FRONT COVER
Then and now. The Ace Cafe in the 1960s . . . and during the re-opening celebrations in 2001. (Museum of London/*After the Battle*)

INSIDE COVERS
'They died for their love of speed.' Pages from the memorial album donated to Mark Wilsmore by *After the Battle* in September 2001.

FRONTSPIECE
Racing on the North Circular in the 1960s. On the right Patsy Gurhy on the back of Rob's Vincent. (Museum of London)

PHOTOGRAPHS
All photographs copyright *After the Battle* save for the following: **Associated Press:** 138 bottom. **BBC:** 88. **Brent Archive:** 155. **James A. Brimble, ARPS:** 13 top. **Camera Press:** 134 bottom right. **Barry Cheese:** 34 top, 36 top, 40 top left, 46 top, 47 left, 50 top right, 57 left, 140 top, 148 both, 149 both. *Classic Bike:* 152, 153 all, 170 right. **Mike Clay:** 140 bottom, 142 top, 145 top left, 160 top right. **Mike Cook:** 137 bottom right. **Martin Craig:** 150. **Tony Evans:** 172 top left. **59 Club:** 137 bottom left. **Gordon Films Inc. New York:** 143 bottom left and right, 124 top left, bottom left, 125 top right, 126 top, middle and bottom left, 127 top right, 128 top, middle and bottom left, 129 top and bottom left, 161 top right, 168 top left and right, 169 left and right. **Harrow Observer:** 157 both. **Highways Agency:** 147. **Hulton Archive:** 62, 104, 108, 109 all, 114 both, 133 top and bottom left. **John Gillett:** 64 top left and right. **Imperial War Museum:** 28. **Arthur Ingram:** 6, 97 top, 122 top, 123 top. **Ron Jamieson:** 99 top, 101 top left. **London Metropolitan Archives:** 17 top, 18 top, 19 top, 20, 24 top, 26 top, 27 bottom. **Museum of London:** 37, 38, 39 both, 40 bottom, 43 top left, 45, 50 top left, 52, 56, 67, 68 top and bottom left, 69 top, 70, 71, 78, 79 top, 81, 82-83, 98 top left, 102, 103, 115, 120, 141. **National Monuments Record Centre:** 151 both, 154. **Popperfoto:** 60, 66, 116, 117 right. **Tony Purbrick:** 74 top, 75, 80, 93 top left and right. **Rev. William Shergold:** 105 left, 106, 107, 110, 111 both, 112, 113, 117 top left, 118 bottom right, 132 top, 137 top. **Simmons Aerofilms:** 31/72, 146. **W. Simmonds:** 14 bottom left. **Maggie Spalding:** 172 top right, bottom left. **Johnny Stuart:** 160 top left, 161 left. **William Wanstall:** 14 top left. **Charlie Williams:** 144, 172 bottom right. **John Willis:** 89-90 (text). **Jenny Wittich:** 84 top, 174 bottom, 175 both.

ACKNOWLEDGEMENTS
The source of all extracts is quoted where known and the Editor apologies for any errors or omissions while extending his grateful acknowledgement to authors and editors of the publications concerned.

Many people contributed material, information, photographs, their valuable time or assistance, and the Editor extends his warm appreciation to: Colin Aish, Nick Baldwin, Henry Bander of TRL Ltd, Brian Baxter, Russell Beharrie, Roger Bell, Marty Black, Francis Blake, Tom Bland of Abbott Mead Vickers BBDO Ltd, Barry Cheese, Michael F. Cook, Martin Craig, Roger Dicken, Steve Earl of the Metropolitan Police Museum, Bryn Elliott, Clare Ellis of the Metropolitan Police, Tony Evans, John Gillett, Richard Gordon of Gordon Films Inc., Gary Hall of the 59 Club, Jacqui Harris from Emap Automotive Ltd, Arthur Ingram, Ron Jamieson, Jennifer Jenkins, Ian Johnson of the Brent Archive, Karen McCall and Merlin Unwin of *London Police Pensioner*, Mark Metcalfe, Geoff O'Neill of *Truckstop News*, Robin Pearson of Nynehead Books, Fred Pentney of Jukeboxes Unlimited, Patsy Pidgeon, Tony Purbrick, Cecil Richards, Michael Robinson, The Rev. William Shergold, Jane Skagman of Mortons Motorcycle Media Ltd, Maggie Spalding, Malcolm Thorne of the National Motor Museum, Charlie Williams, Yvonne Williams, John Willis and Jenny Wittich.

Editorial note

During the period in which the Ace became a motorcycling mecca — roughly the mid-1950s to the mid-1960s — hundreds of bikers regularly used this transport cafe on London's North Circular Road as a pit-stop. All will have their own tales to relate . . . their own experiences to recount . . . and their own special memories of those days, which is why I have chosen to let one of the boys who was there set the scene for us and tell it the way it was. Barry Cheese, better known under his nickname of 'Noddy', was one of the main ringleaders and was present at the Ace on virtually every single night during what he calls 'the Golden Years'. He saw it all first hand and his recollections make fascinating reading.

Noddy's account is then set beside the wider picture, as told through the press reports of the time. The story ends with Mark Wilsmore's epic seven-year venture to acquire and re-convert the building back to reflect an important part of British history and culture.

In those days, motorcyclists were constantly in the headlines because they were killing themselves in increasing numbers, despite the efforts of the police to stop them. Since 1928 when our story begins, 75,000 motorcyclists have lost their lives on the roads of Britain, at least five of whom, listed within these pages, died within yards of each other on the North Circular in the vicinity of the Ace: David Foster, Bobby Owen, Kathleen Keane, Bob Griffiths and Dave Lambert.

This book is dedicated to them and all those who have died through their love of riding on two wheels . . . and through their love of speed.

WINSTON RAMSEY, EDITOR-IN CHIEF, *AFTER THE BATTLE*, 2002

Contents

INTRODUCTION:
    'DE-LUXE CAFE — COFFEE STALL PRICES'   6

IN THE BEGINNING . . .   8

THE NORTH CIRCULAR ROAD   18

THE ACE AT STONEBRIDGE PARK   26

THE WAY IT WAS THEN . . .
    MEMORIES OF A BOY RACER   32

THE GOLDEN YEARS   60

THE TWILIGHT YEARS   138

RESURRECTION   146

Introduction: 'De-Luxe Cafe — Coffee Stall Prices'

Two recently opened and newly appointed Bedford Drivers Club rest houses illustrate far more effectively than words the improvements made in the transport workers' 'hotel' — the Ace Cafe at Stonebridge Park and the Kempsey Cafe and Service Station just outside Worcester.

The Ace Cafe stands alongside the North Circular Road, with a frontage of 350 feet, and one of the largest lorry parks in the country. It is centrally heated, and the toilets (ladies are catered for as well as gentlemen) are provided with hot and cold water.

The kitchen, tiled throughout, is fitted with the sort of equipment that would delight the chef of a luxury restaurant. Everything is planned for quick service, and in a recent time test 92 customers were served with lunch in nine minutes.

All told, there is seating accommodation for 110 drivers, and meals are served at any hour of the day or night.

There is also a spacious games room in which customers can amuse themselves with cards, darts, bar billiards and other games provided by the management.

Owners will be interested to know that the Bedford Drivers Club scheme of 'communications' has been adopted in the cafe. Any employer who wishes to get into touch with his driver may telephone a message to the cafe and have that message placed on a notice board for the driver to see when he arrives.

The site, the building and the equipment cost £10,000. Yet the prices charged are more than reasonable — in actual fact, the same as those prevailing in ordinary coffee stalls.

Since the Bedford Drivers Club was launched a few years ago, it has become well known as one of the most important drivers' welfare organisations in the country.

One of its most ambitious schemes was the inauguration of a network of rest houses all over the country — roadside transport cafes in which members of the club are assured of parking space, good food, cheerful service and clean beds.

None of these rest houses is allowed to exhibit the B.D.C. sign until it has been inspected and approved by officials of the club. A long and tedious job, but one which ensures that the sign is something more than a sheet of enamelled iron.

In other words, a B.D.C. rest house is now accepted as a *good* rest house. And the Bedford Drivers Club means to maintain that reputation. From now on, all approved rest house appointments will be automatically cancelled every two years.

Those which are still up to the standard set by the club will be reinstated. Those which have dropped below that standard since they were appointed will have to mend their ways or drop out.

This move, incidentally, has been welcomed by nearly all of the five hundred rest houses now on the list. The proprietors realise that it is in their interests to set and maintain a high level of cleanliness and catering, and to do everything possible to establish the B.D.C. appointment as a symbol of good service.

Gone are the days when a coffee stall or a galvanised iron shack represented the best that a driver could expect in the way of road pull-ups. The driver has benefited, and so has the owner — because it has meant increased efficiency as well as a saving of time, and the ability to plan long-distance schedules while still observing the statutory hours law.

The Bedford Transport Magazine, March 1939

Then . . . and now. Built in 1938 . . . bombed in 1940 . . . rebuilt in 1948 . . . closed in 1969. The Ace Cafe on London's North Circular Road has enjoyed a colourful history, its 'Golden Years' being from the mid-1950s to the mid-1960s when it became a motorcycling mecca. In its infamous heyday, the North Circular between Neasden and Hangar Lane became an unofficial race-track with nightly 'burn-ups' between the teenage 'ton-up' boys who used the Ace as their pit-stop. After it closed, the building was used for many years as a tyre-fitting depot until its resurrection in 2001 when hundreds of motorcyclists, nostalgic for the legend of the Ace, gathered on a beautiful weekend in September to celebrate its re-opening.

The thrill of racing at speed on motorcycles was born in Britain on Sunday, February 19, 1928. Although an earlier meeting is recorded as having taken place during the previous year at Manchester, it was that first dirt-track race which fired the imagination of the public and attracted huge crowds to High Beech in Epping Forest, north-east of London.

In the beginning . . .

Since the beginning of time the lure of speed has fascinated human beings . . . Centuries ago, in the days of the Caesars, enormous crowds were thrilled by the great chariot races which satisfied the public craving for excitement.

The modern equivalent of the sport of the ancient Romans is dirt-track racing. Here is the sport that satisfies the inherent public demand for speed and at the same time provides the tremendously more important human element.

Norman Pritchard,
Speedway News, May 19, 1928

Over 3,000 people flocked here today to watch the first DTM races held in this country. There were thrills in plenty, motorcyclists tearing around the track with their knees almost touching the ground and, in some cases, landing on their heads when their machines skidded from under them. But the enormous size of the crowd which gathered at the King's Oak Speedway provided the greatest surprise of all.

The races were timed to run from 10.30 until 4.30 and there were eight events with several 'heats' in each race. With such a feast of thrills offered, motorcyclists turned up in their thousands while motorists and others rolled up through the day. Considerable difficulty was found in accommodating this huge crowd of spectators, owing to the danger of being run into by the machines, are supposed to be confined to the inside of the track only. As this was impossible, even the hundreds of stewards present, could not restrain the enthusiastic crowds from crossing the track and watching from the outside. Those who desired a 'grandstand' view climbed trees where, both in clambering and swinging from the branches, they supplied as many thrills as the motorcyclists, to the huge enjoyment of the crowd.

Two Australian 'cracks' Mackay and Galoway were competing, all the others being Englishmen who had never ridden on a dirt track before.

Daily Mirror, February 1928

KING'S OAK SPEEDWAY, HIGH BEECH, LOUGHTON, ESSEX

(By kind permission of L. W. E. MARDEN, Esq.)

PROGRAMME of . .

DIRT TRACK RACING

Organised by the ILFORD MOTOR CYCLE & LIGHT CAR CLUB under A.C.U Permit. Restricted to the following Clubs :
Ilford M.C. & L.C.C. and Colchester Motor Club.

SUNDAY, FEBRUARY 19th, 1928, at 10.30 a.m.

Officials :

Eastern Centre Stwd.—M. R.W.Fison, Esq,   *Judges*—E. J. Bass, Esq. (Essex M.C.), C. Baxter, Esq. (Ilford), P. Cox, Esq. (Ilford).
Timekeeper and Starter—Ray Abbot, Esq. (Essex M.C.).
Lap Scorers—O. Verrall, Esq, (Ilford), P, Clifton, Esq, (Colchester),   *Finance*—D, Page, Esq, (Ilford),
Marshals—Members of Clubs,   *Marshal in Charge*—A, Bellamy, Esq, (Ilford),

Spectators must keep to the inner portion of the track behind ropes.	If Competitors fall they must be left to the Marshals. On no account must the public invade the track.
No dogs allowed inside under any consideration.	These rules are laid down by the Governing Body, the Auto-Cycle Union and unless strictly adhered to the
Spectators will only be allowed to cross track between events and at one place only.	Stewards of the Meeting have power to stop this event and also further events.

Please help all you can.   *Thank you !*

ADMISSION SIXPENCE

CAR PARK under supervision.

LUNCHEONS : 4/- (Table d'Hote), 3/-
TEAS, 1/6
These must be booked from the Hotel if wanted.

PROGRAMME TWOPENCE

Cars **6d.**, Cycles and Three-wheelers **3d.**

Hon. Organising Secretary :
R. J. Hill-Bailey,
41, Hickling Road, Ilford.

The programme for the early meetings included the warning: 'The Speedway is at the King's Oak, not on the roads approaching same.'

The Motorcycle Club held a dirt track meeting on Saturday at the King's Oak Speedway, Loughton. Through the agency of the vice-president, Mr W. J. Cearns, the gathering were able to see the Australian cracks, Vic Huxley, who recently broke the world's record, and Cecil Brown, of the USA. The International Speedway arranged for Huxley to travel by air from Naples. Huxley, who had not ridden a machine for three months, and had a strange motor to ride, managed to clip 3-5ths of a second off A. Frogley's record. Frogley did not beat the time set up by Huxley.

The Woodford Times, May 11, 1938

In 1927 or 28, my late brother Jack having been unable to obtain employment in his trade of central heating engineer landed a job labouring with the firm building the speedway.

When he came home every night, my younger brother and I would quiz him for the latest information. I can well remember him coming home and saying Billy Galloway had had a try out on the track.

Fortunately shortly after this my brother obtained work back in his own trade. I think he went to the first meeting. I myself did not go until the summer of 1931. My brother took me, and I can remember being very excited travelling by Acme coach from Hastingwood, where we then lived, and

getting off at the Wake Arms, and walking and running up the road to High Beech, with one or two short cuts through the forest.

High Beech that day was captained by Syd Edmonds, who I think, was a local man. Also in the High Beech team were Jack Barnett, Phil Bishop, and a newcomer newly arrived from Australia, Bobby or Billy Blake, who turned in a pretty good performance.

The match that day was a league versus Lea Bridge, the only rider I can remember was 'Squib' Burton, perhaps because he had a crash and had to have spokes removed from the rear wheel to free his foot.

L. S. Redington, 1984

No doubt part of the thrill was in the spills. Bill Galloway had come to Britain from Australia to demonstrate the sport — something which he certainly achieved that Sunday in a spectacular way!

More than 40 years ago, the roar of a massive coughing engine tore open the silence deep in Epping Forest.

A gang of young men shifted trees, laid down cinders and introduced a new creature to the woods — the motorcycle.

There, at High Beech, Loughton, a quiet corner of the forest was to give birth to a new sport and a crop of young riders who were to become almost legendary.

Credit for that first track goes to Mr. Lionel Wills, then secretary of the Ilford and District Motorcycling Club. He heard from Australia of an activity called dirt track racing.

A friend supplied graphic details of the sport and said it was exciting, lots of fun — and highly dangerous.

Mr. Wills went to the King's Oak, High Beech. He knew that nearby, tucked in the trees, was a small running track falling into disuse.

With a little extending here and there, some cinders, a few trees removed and some eager motorcyclists, a trial could begin, he thought.

After preparation, he announced the meeting and invited any prospective motorcycling dare-devils along to High Beech. By Easter 1928 crowds of 20,000 were gathering to see Speedway.

Later, High Beech, the first milestone in the exciting history of British Speedway, fell into disrepair. Ponies occasionally came along for small shows, but little else happened. Silver birches sprang up on the banks and poked through the roof of the old wooden grandstand. Grass covered the cinders.

And that is how it remained until a few weeks ago, when the last traces of the circuit were removed to create a field study centre for the Corporation of London. What once echoed to the roar of motorcycles has, perhaps rightfully, been restored to nature.

Guardian & Gazette, January 1, 1971

From racing circuit to conservation centre . . . yet High Beech still retains its unique place in the hearts of motorcyclists.

At this time of the year members of the Veteran Dirt Track Riders' Association get down to reliving 'the good old days' usually with a dinner-dance. That annual event was held last Saturday. On Sunday they'll all be trooping up to High Beech, near Loughton, to relive the memories of the first-ever meeting behind the King's Oak, which took place almost 40 years to the day — on Sunday, February 19th, 1928.

Stars of the sport — past, present and future — are all expected to gather in the heart of Epping Forest on Sunday for a big programme of events which will include displays of most of the leading trophies ever competed for in Speedway. Secretary Peter Arnold has also arranged for displays of programmes, pictures and badges. 'In fact,' says Peter, 'nostalgia by the bucketful.'

One of the leading personalities to have a place of honour in the Cavalcade of Speedway, which gets under way at 2.15 p.m., will be Johnnie S. Hoskins. It was in November 1923 that Johnnie first started the Speedway bug as a special attraction for one of his agricultural shows in Newcastle, Australia.

It promises to be a great day, reserved in the main for the veterans of the sport. One thing is for certain, though, it will be an autograph-hunter's paradise!

Guardian & Gazette, February 16, 1968

Historic reunion on the track in February 1968 — the 40th anniversary of the first race. *Above:* **Ready to go are Phil Bishop, Jack Barnett and Sonny Wilson.** *Below:* **Geoff Pymar, Alex Slow, Fred Law, George Gower with Cyril Taft on the bike.**

There has been a surprise 'bonus' for the High Beech Green Belt Association in its struggle to preserve the calm of Epping Forest.

Without any persuasion by forest-lovers, Chigwell Council has decided to close off part of Fairmead Bottom to traffic. This will leave one of the more beautiful roads through the forest undisturbed by the roar of cars and the smell of exhaust fumes.

Actually the road will be closed only from its junction with Epping New Road as far as Palmers Bridge, but this will remove traffic from the forest where it disturbs the natural surroundings, and divert it back on to the A11.

The council made its decision after pressure was brought to bear by Essex County Council in view of the hazards involved in traffic turning right at the junction.

West Essex Gazette, February 1, 1974

High Beech motorcyclists have been effectively told to 'buzz off' by Epping Forest Council.

Chingford police had asked the council to take action on problems caused by many motorcyclists congregating on Sundays and Bank Holidays in the King's Oak area of High Beech.

The triangular section of road in front of the King's Oak is being used as a race track and the police have asked that one side of the triangle should be experimentally closed to stop this.

So last week's meeting of the transportation committee councillors agreed to authorise district secretary Peter Snelling to make and seal the Epping Forest (Queen's Green, High Beech) (Experimental Prohibition of Driving) Order.

He has been authorised to give notice of the making of the order according to statutory regulations and the order will last for 18 months.

Guardian & Gazette, June 7, 1985

Motorcyclists are claiming that an experimental prohibition of driving order is a plot to exclude them from the High Beech area.

The motorcyclists have launched a petition to protest against the experimental prohibition of driving in Queen's Green, opposite the King's Oak pub, in High Beech.

The track may have been lost but the roads through the Forest — particularly Fairmead Bottom *(above)* **— were attractive replacements.**

The protesters claim there are plans to exclude all motorcyclists from High Beech.

The petition, containing 225 signatures of motorcyclists who congregate in the High Beech area, has been submitted to Epping Forest Council.

Guardian & Gazette, November 22, 1985

But road closures, and policemen — of the real and sleeping variety — put paid to local speed trials yet bikers seeking the nostalgia of former years still congregate at the tea hut at the end of Fairmead Bottom.

From High Beech . . . to the North Circular. The Epping New Road, built in 1830-34 to cut out the steep hills in and out of Loughton, which caused so much suffering to horse-drawn traffic in earlier times, has claimed many lives. One of the most tragic motorcycle deaths in recent years occurred in October 1978 when a young soldier going on leave to visit his family collided with a lorry between Rangers Road and the Robin Hood, not far from the Fairmead Bottom junction *(above)* which was closed off in 1974. He now lies buried in High Beech churchyard; another victim of the 'Murder Mile'.

Tarmacadam and arterial roads banish romance, but new knowledge has been brought to bear on old problems and perhaps there is some consolation in the modern changes if they have brought nearer a realisation of that prophet's vision that 'A highway shall be there and a way . . . and the unclean shall not pass over it but it shall be for those the wayfaring men who, though fools, shall not err therein.

R. J. Rumsey, December 11, 1933

A notorious accident black spot, a roundabout was added to the junction at the Robin Hood during reconstruction in 1936.

Each motorcycling generation talks about what they consider to be, at least in their mind, a Golden Age of motorcycling. I wish sometimes that it were possible to transport the young riders of today back in a form of time machine, however. They would find things very much warmer in composition, and the harshness that accompanies this violent age would be non-existent. The twenties were adventurous years and one cannot help but feel very nostalgic when one thinks of those famous motorcycle clubs and the activities that went on within 'The Kilburn and District', 'The London Eagles', 'The Bayswater', and many others.

In those days Reg and Kelly Bounds with friends would congregate outside the Grange Cinema, Kilburn. The usual items of dress were Fair Isle pullovers, Bedford cord breeches, natty little scarves and lace-up boots just like the TT riders wore. Five or six of the bloods would race up and down the Kilburn High Road on their sporty machines, looking for any local talent. During this bit of investigation, the local policeman would

The Golden Age of motorcycling; those happy carefree days before the war with no restrictions, no licences . . . and no speed limits! *Above:* **Jimmy, Eric, Gordon, Jack and Dick pull up for a breather with a BSA and two Levis's.** *Below:* **Eric, another BSA aficionado, takes Blanche for a trip to the seaside on the much-loved Sloper.**

have been alerted to what was going on. The outcome of this little matter being that these examples of Britain's wild youth were informed that, 'I know ye'r fathers and I've got ye'r numbers everyone of ye'r'. The little group of sportsmen then moved off to Hampstead Heath, shouting in the wind as they went that the last one up Netherhall Gardens was a sissy. On arriving at Spaniards Road, all the old business started again where perhaps some of the talent from NW3 would deign to jump on the pillion of a machine or two. The pack would then move off for a spot of unofficial hill-climbing at Brockley Hill. That only one member of the party possessed any form of lighting was of little consequence as they sped back into Kilburn, a little convoy trailing behind the only chap with the lights.

Denis Howard, 1973

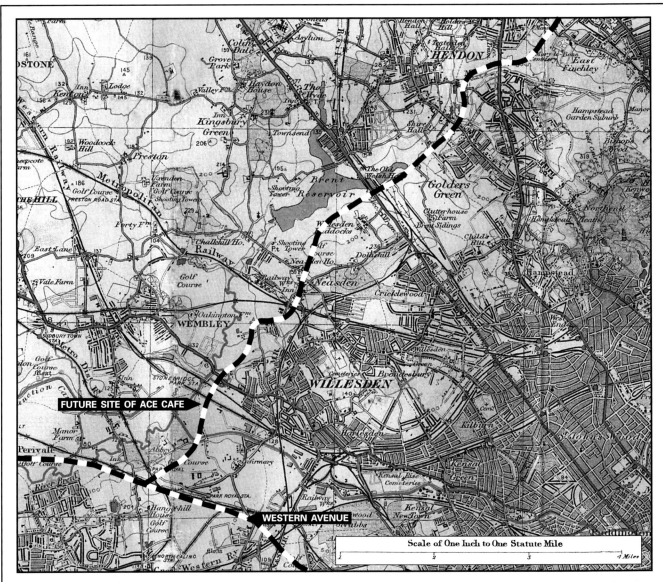

FUTURE SITE OF ACE CAFE

WESTERN AVENUE

Scale of One Inch to One Statute Mile

And it is still from High Beech that enthusiastic bikers set off on a pilgrimage . . . a pilgrimage which rolls back the years to the heady days of the 1950s when the North Circular Road became a focal point for a new breed of young men on two wheels.

But first the road had to be built. The map shows north London as it was in 1921. The route of the yet-to-be-built North Circular is dotted as is the line of the Western Avenue which was to bring relief to the road from London to Oxford.

When the Ministry of Transport became the central authority on roads, it was decided to allot certain monies, notably the revenue derived from the taxes on motor vehicles, to the maintenance of the roads. To ensure that the greatest benefits were gained by those roads which bear, so to speak, the national traffic, as apart from those roads which carry purely local traffic and which, therefore, justly look for their upkeep to local resources, it was found necessary to classify the roads all over the country. The roads have accordingly been classified in three categories, viz.:—

1st Class Roads, 2nd Class Roads, Other Roads.

The 1st Class Roads are the great arterial routes connecting London and Edinburgh with the large towns and the large towns with one another. The 2nd Class Roads (which are smaller, less important, but still important), consisting of roads connecting smaller towns with the 1st class roads. The other, or 3rd class roads are maintained by purely local funds.

Having classified the roads, a system was established by which each individual road, or part of a road, could be identified as part of a route. Roads are designated as follows:—

1st Class Roads are identified by the letter 'A', 2nd Class Roads are identified by the letter 'B'. Finally, all 1st and 2nd Class roads are numbered.

Originally a single carriageway for much of its length, this picture of the Finchley section of the North Circular was taken in September 1934 looking west.

For the purpose of numbering the roads, Great Britain has been divided into nine sectors, six of which radiate in clockwise order from London, and the remaining three similarly from Edinburgh. These great arterial highways — A1, A2, A3, A4, A5, A6, A7, A8 and A9 — are: A1 London to Edinburgh, A2 London to Dover, A3 London to Portsmouth, A4 London to Bath, A5 London to Holyhead, A6 London to Carlisle, A7 Edinburgh to Carlisle, A8 Edinburgh to Gourock, A9 Edinburgh to Inverness.

Michelin Guide to Great Britain, 1925

The same view 67 years later. The wide grass verges permitted the easy addition of a second carriageway.

The North Circular Road

Then and now at the junction at Hendon with the Great North Way which was given the classification 'A1' when the Ministry of Transport became responsible for Britain's roads in 1919.

The earliest roads in England were tracks made by the ancient Britons and in Middlesex there is evidence of three of these, all of which commenced at the great ford across the Thames near Brentford.

The first led eastwards through the districts known today as Strand-on-the-Green, Chiswick, Fulham, and Chelsea to Charing Cross; the second ran between Hanwell and Ealing over Horsendon and Sudbury Hills to Brockley Hill at Stanmore, where there was an encampment, and the third went by way of Hanwell and Hayes to the ford across the River Colne at Uxbridge.

When the Romans colonised Britain, they constructed a network of military roads, solidly built of stone on good foundations, and three of these pass through the county: Ermine

Looking back east towards Regents Park Road.

TURNPIKES AND TOLLS

General conditions, however, remained deplorable and during the 17th century Parliament, with what was tantamount to a confession of failure in dealing with the matter, allowed toll and turnpike roads to come into existence.

The toll bridge was a familiar sight in the Middle Ages but the turnpike system proper, by which barriers were placed across a road and tolls taken from all but pedestrians and a few privileged travellers, dates from 1663 when Parliament, on petition of a number of justices, authorised the erection of toll barriers along the Great North Road.

The system spread very rapidly, so that by 1770 there were over 1,100 Turnpike Trusts, administering 23,000 miles of road, with 7,800 toll-gates and employing 20,000 pikemen to collect the tolls. The system was unpopular although turnpike roads were generally better than others.

Street (the route of which is followed today by the Hertford Road as far as Edmonton), running from Bishopsgate through Tottenham and Waltham Cross to Lincoln; Watling Street, following the route now taken by the Edgware Road from Marble Arch to where it leaves the county to the north of Brockley Hill for Hertfordshire; and a third leading from London through Shepherd's Bush, Chiswick, Brentford, Hounslow and Staines to Silchester, along the route now taken by the Staines Road.

Someone had to be made responsible for their upkeep and in 1555 an Act of Parliament was passed establishing a principle which remained in operation for three hundred years. This Act decreed that each parish was responsible for the maintenance of the roads through it and for the supply of the necessary labour and materials.

From 1935 . . . to 2001. The convent visible through the trees behind the leading lorry in the pre-war photo still exists.

West of the Edgware Road — the old Roman Watling Street — the North Circular became dual carriageway, this photo being taken just beyond in June 1934. We are looking back east towards Staples & Co, the bedding manufacturers, in the far distance.

MAIN ROADS

'Main Roads', as a new class of road, were created by the Highway and Locomotive Amendment Act 1878. These roads included all roads which had ceased to be turnpike roads after 1870 and any other roads which were considered to be of sufficient importance by reason of their being the principal means of communication between towns, or thoroughfares leading to railway stations. One half of the cost of the maintenance of these main roads was placed upon the county and the other half was borne by the local authorities.

The first attempt made by the Government to take executive control over the roads was the formation of the Road Board in 1909, with the passing of the Development and Road Improve-ment Funds Act. The Board was empowered to make grants of money to local governing bodies for the purpose of improving existing roads and constructing new ones. The creation of this body marked the recognition by the Government of the advent of a new era of life on the roads.

The Board continued in existence until 1919 when it was superseded by the Ministry of Transport, formed by Act of Parliament in that year to deal with railways, tramways, waterways, roads, bridges, harbours and docks. Under this Act, also, first- and second-class roads were created, a percentage of the cost of maintenance and improvement of which, varying according to the class of road, was to be borne by the Ministry of Transport.

ARTERIAL ROADS

By far the greatest problem, particularly around London, was the provision and design of roads adequate to cope with the increasing amount of traffic using them. In 1912 the Local Government Board appointed a Departmental Committee to consider what improved means of road communication were necessary for the metropolis and, as a result, proposals for constructing new roads, to be called 'arterial' roads, were recommended.

Before any of these proposals could be put in hand the 1914-18 war had broken out and the commencement of the works was postponed until 1920 when the County Council obtained the authority of the Ministry of Transport to the construction of various sections of these roads as a means of relieving the heavy unemployment which followed the demobilisation of the Forces. From then until the outbreak of the next war in 1939, the following schemes were amongst those carried out for Middlesex:

1. The Cambridge Road, designed to relieve the already serious congestion along the roads running in a northerly direction through the eastern part of the County, from Tottenham, through Edmonton and Enfield.

2. The North Circular Road, planned to relieve London as far as possible of traffic intending to cross, rather than enter it, to intersect and connect every main road converging on London through Middlesex. It commenced at the junction of the Great West Road and Chiswick High Road, runs northwards and eastwards through Chiswick, Acton, Ealing, Wembley, Willesden, Hendon, Finchley, Friern Barnet, Hornsey, Southgate and Edmonton, and passes into Essex via Chingford.

3. Western Avenue intended as a by-pass to the London-Oxford Road between Marble Arch and Uxbridge, was planned to commence just west of thc Egware Road at Paddington, pass through North Hammersmith, entering the county at Old Oak Common Lane, Acton, and to proceed almost due west through Acton, Park Royal, Perivale, Greenford, Northolt and Harefield to its termination near Denham. The viaduct, some 1,600ft in length, over the Colne Valley was begun in 1939.

Coles Green Road, off the opposite carriageway in between the plate-glass works of Shepherd Tobias and Scribbans-Kemp's bakery, is still there, although the pillar box, visible in the pre-war photograph beside the second lorry, has gone with the construction of the flyover. We still refer to this as Staples Corner although the original firm has long gone!

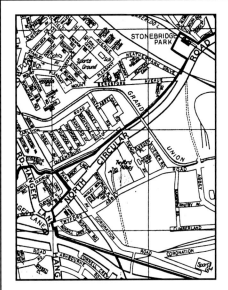

At Twyford at its western end, an aquaduct had to be built to carry the Grand Union Canal over the road.

4. The Great West Road, designed to commence at Cromwell Road, West Kensington, and to bypass Hammersmith Broadway and the High Streets of Chiswick, Brentford and Hounslow, and to terminate at the Bath Road, west of Hounslow.

5. The Chertsey Road, planned to relieve traffic to the south-west, commences in Chiswick High Road. It crosses the Thames at Chiswick and again at Twickenham, where new bridges were built in 1933.

6. The Watford Bypass was constructed from Finchley Road to the County boundary near Aldenham Reservoir.

7. The Barnet Bypass runs from the junction of Archway Road and North Hill, Highgate, to the County boundary about two miles north of Mimms Hall in South Mimms.

Before the war, the aqueduct had been a target for an IRA bomb which caused a leak on the northern side which was never successfully repaired. When this section of the North Circular was due to be upgraded in the early 1990s, Balfour Beatty had the tricky job of widening the bridge. The canal could only be closed for a limited period so, at the tendering stage, the company proposed an alternative design whereby the new aqueduct was constructed to one side and slid into position during the canal closure period. This method greatly reduced the complexity of the project. This picture was taken from the rooftop of the Katsouris food factory on New Year's Day 2002.

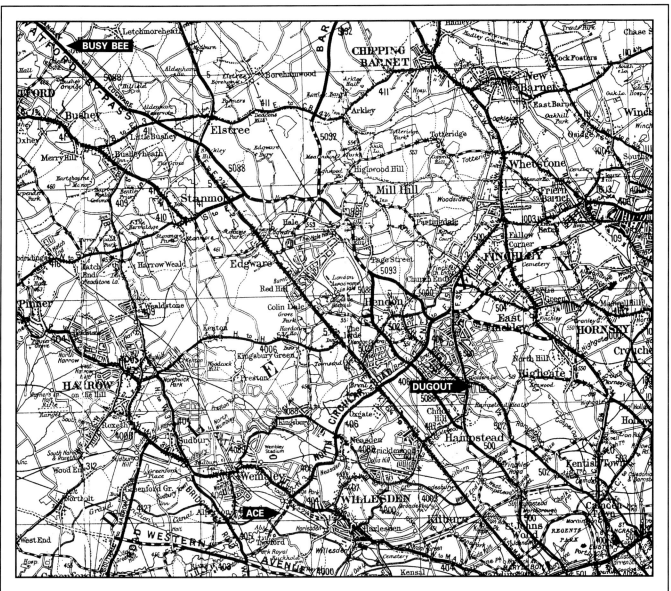

Termination of the 15-mile North Circular Road — the A406 — was at Hangar Lane where it met the Western Avenue — the A40. Bacon's pre-war Motor Road Map was specially produced to show the routes of the new arterial roads and bypasses around London although the dotted sections have yet to be built. Locations which feature in our story have been arrowed.

Before the war, the Western Avenue-Hangar Lane junction was simply controlled by traffic lights (which had first appeared in Britain in 1927), but as the volume of traffic increased and accidents mounted, a scheme was initiated in 1958-61 for the construction of an underpass for the Western Avenue with pedestrian subways to aid road safety.

ROAD SAFETY

Concurrently with the construction of these new roads, Middlesex County Council executed extensive schemes for the widening and improvement of most of the old roads and many of the bridges in the county. These involved the provision of dual carriageways to accommodate local and standing traffic; the installation of systems of automatic traffic signals or, where space has permitted, the construction of traffic 'roundabouts' at important road junctions; the provision of pedestrian subways; the provision of super elevation or 'banking' on curves to lessen the danger from skidding; and, lastly, the provision of a multiplicity of traffic signs and road-markings to make the highway safer for motorist and pedestrian alike.

In 1970, a massive new 'gyratory' road system was introduced which altered the layout of the junction yet again, creating frequent bottlenecks.

On numerous occasions the new roads have been criticized from the point of view of their barren ugliness as compared with the leafy lanes of yesterday. The County Council is making every effort to make its roads as beautiful as they are efficient. Grass verges are laid out at the sides and avenues of young trees and flowering shrubs are planted along them, the County Council having its own nurseries, staffed by horticultural experts, for this purpose.

Middlesex, Sir Clifford Radcliffe, 1949

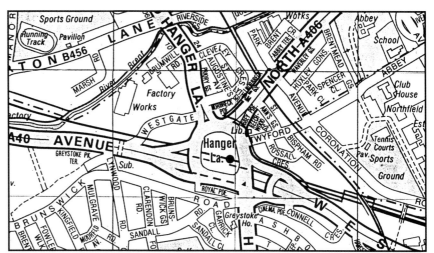

In August 1931, the first sods were being cut in Stonebridge Park to drive the North Circular through to Park Royal. The beginnings of the carriageway can be seen being laid down in the middle distance.

Willesden heads the list for road casualties in the London area — 'the blackest district', said the headline. In the first 34 weeks of the year there were 750 casualties. In the week ending August 24, 24 people were injured, as compared with 26 in the previous week.

Press report, 1935

A movement was on foot among residents to persuade the Minister of Transport to impose a 30 m.p.h. speed limit on the North Circular Road, between Neasden Roundabout and Staples Corner. The paper pointed out that there had been a large number of accidents here, some fatal.

Willesden Chronicle, September 1935

Ace Cafe Ltd, North Circular Road, NW10. ELGar 6491.

Kelly's Post Office Directory, 1949

The Ace at Stonebridge Park

Can this really be the same place? Our comparison taken in September 2001 is almost unbelievable!

SPEED LIMITS STILL IN FORCE

At Witham Petty Session last week Mr. G. C. Benham, Colchester, who appeared for a defendant in a speed limit case, said there was an impression that under the new Road Traffic Act all speed limits were done away with. This was not so, as, under an obscure section of the Act, speed limits would continue to be enforced for another twelve months, or longer, if the Minister of Transport so decided.

The Chairman, Mr. Collingwood Hope, K.C.: 'That applies not only to motor cars, but to every form of motor traffic?' Mr. Benham: 'Yes, sir.'

The Chairman said he hoped the Press would kindly notice that, in the interests of motorists generally. 'These speed limits are not abolished in areas where they previously existed,' he said.

Woodford Times, January 16, 1931

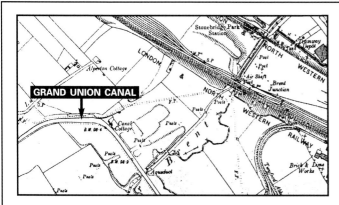

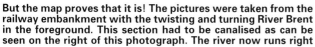

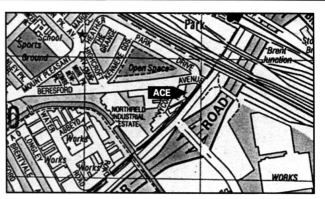

But the map proves that it is! The pictures were taken from the railway embankment with the twisting and turning River Brent in the foreground. This section had to be canalised as can be seen on the right of this photograph. The river now runs right behind the site where the Ace transport cafe was built seven years later. By an odd coincidence, the first roadhouse built in Britain was another Ace — the Ace of Spades on the Great West Road at Hounslow which had opened its doors in 1926.

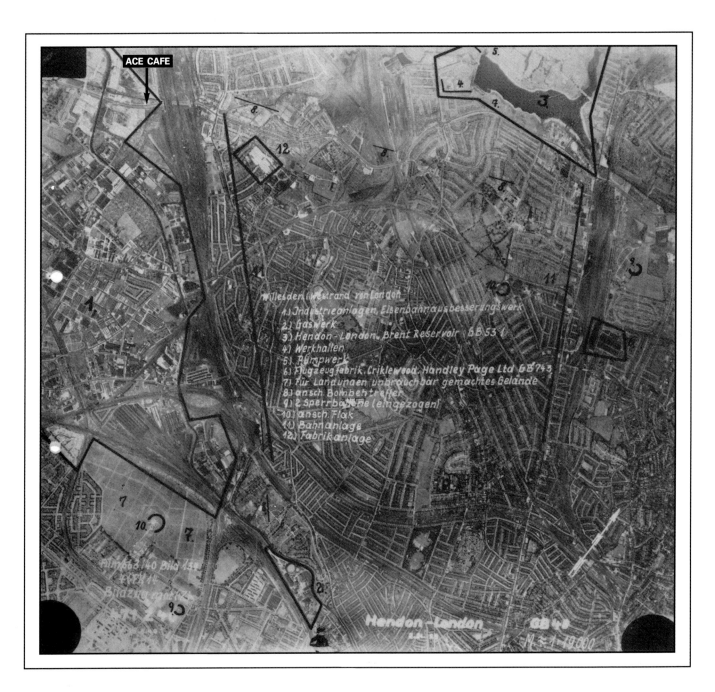

ACE CAFE

Willesden (Westrand von London)
1.) Industrieanlagen, Eisenbahnausbesserungswerk
2.) Gaswerk
3.) Hendon - London, Brent Reservoir GB 53 l
4.) Werkhallen
5.) Pumpwerk
6.) Flugzeugfabrik, Cricklewood, Handley Page Ltd GB 743
7.) für Landungen unbrauchbar gemachtes Gelände
8.) ansch Bombentreffer
9.) 2 Sperrballone (eingezogen)
10.) ansch Flak
11.) Bahnanlage
12.) Fabrikanlage

Hendon - London   GB 48
M ≈ 1 : 19 000

No sooner had the cafe been opened than the Second World War began. The Luftwaffe had already prepared its target maps with the intention of singling out key points — called Zielgebiete — for attack. The Hendon area *(opposite)* with its concentration of aviation, transportation and industrial targets was high on the priority list and the Ace (arrowed by us), right alongside the Willesden railway complex, was very vulnerable. The worst incident to affect the area was caused by a specialist unit — the 3rd Gruppe of Kampfgeschwader 26 — carrying a new bomb, the 2½-ton SC 2500 *(right)*. The specially adapted Heinkel 111s carried the massive bomb, dubbed 'Max' by the British, externally, and were guided to their targets by the top secret Y-Verfaren navigation radio beam. And only two crews were cleared to carry the bomb to Britain. Victoria Station received the first Max on the night of December 21/22, 1940 followed by the Royal Naval Dockyard at Portsmouth on the 23/24th. Both bombs missed their targets by a few hundred yards. *Above:* Hendon received its Max on the night of February 13/14, 1941.

The Max was still a relatively new weapon in the Luftwaffe's armoury and would not have been deliberately dropped on civilians. The navigation beams would have been locked onto a military target of some importance in the area — most probably the de Havilland plant (Target GB 73 33) in Stag Lane, Edgware. On this occasion the crew of III/KG26 who dropped the SC 2500 after a flight of 200 miles from their base at Poix came within 3,000 yards of hitting their target. The bomb exploded on the alleyway between the back gardens of Nos. 50-52 Ravenstone Road and 51-53 Borthwick Road, totally destroying 84 houses and badly damaging another 160. In all, over 750 properties were affected by blast and over 600 persons made homeless. The death toll recorded by the Civil Defence historian after the war stated that 75 people lost their lives but local records indicate 80 with 148 hospital cases and 300 more slightly injured. *Above:* On February 23 a memorial service was held and a cross of rememberance, made out of charred timbers, erected on the site.

After the war, Argyle Road was completely demolished, the broken spurs of Ramsey, Borthwick and Ravenstone only remaining to mark Hendon's greatest tragedy.

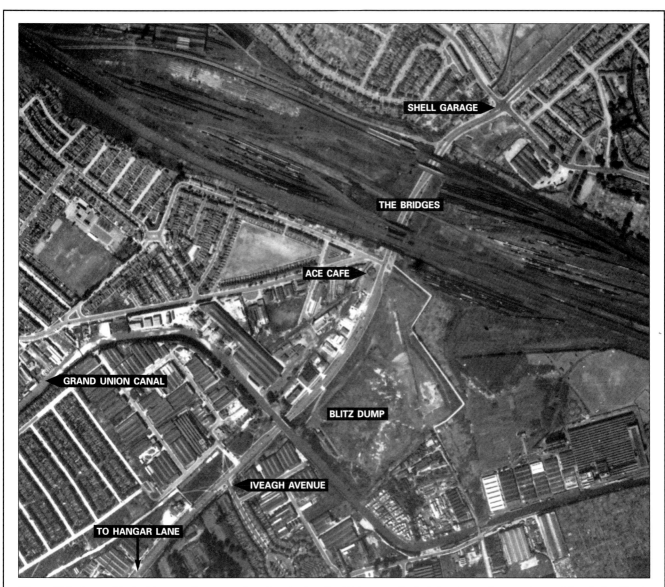

The rubble from this incident and many other hundreds of wrecked houses and factories across north-west London was brought to a site opposite the Ace, itself a victim to the bombing in 1940. The massive heap of debris, some 50 feet high, stretched right along the southern side of the North Circular up to the Grand Union Canal. This picture taken in June 1949 shows the rebuilt café. Soon, it was to enjoy its enduring moment of glory.

During the late 1950s and early 60s, Barry Cheese spent virtually all his leisure time at the Ace and when he was not acting as one of the ringleaders, he was being an eyewitness to most of the escapades which took place there. He was a thorn in the side of the law but in the countless burn-ups on 'the Circular' — all helmetless — he only came a cropper twice with minor injuries. Barry still lives in Willesden where he showed us this cafe trophy from what he calls 'the Golden Years'.

The way it was then . . . memories of a boy racer

I was born in Notting Hill in 1939 — 23rd July — a rough area but it was friendly. Things were rationed as it was wartime yet everyone helped each other. Times were bad yet it was a great time. My dad Stan had been wounded in North Africa with the RAF and he died before the war ended. So my mum had to bring up my sister and myself on her own. She used to do three jobs — morning cleaning, working in a bakery during the day, and more cleaning at night.

We had no bath so on Saturdays we used to go to the baths for what we called our 'annual'. It cost 2d but if you wanted to be posh and turn your own hot and cold water on you could have a 6d special although we could not afford it.

After the war we used to play on bomb sites. There were horse and carts on the streets — totters, rag fairs (nowadays they would be called boot fairs — and my mum always went because all she could afford were second hand clothes. The other things in our lives then were

the tally man and the pawn shop — and I don't mean telly and porno!

I first went to school in a converted church hall in Lancaster Road — a Jewish school where I got both the Jewish and Christian holidays. There were times when I couldn't go to school because I had no shoes — Mum had the coupons but no money. When I was 11 I went to St John's School in Clarendon Road but I had a lot of time off to help my mum and left before I was 15 in 1954.

Typical early post-war scene at the Ace, pictured from the mound of Blitz rubble with the carriageways split with traffic islands.

I used to work part-time in a butcher's shop and I carried on full-time when I left school for a while but didn't really like the job and I drifted, trying to find my vocation. I used to help my uncle with his motorbike, stripping it down, handing him tools and the like, and began to get very interested. There were lots of ex-Servicemen around and he used to go to the Ace which was then just a transport café and meeting place on what was an important route round London. It didn't have the reputation that it did during the golden years which lasted from 1958 to 1962.

I was keen to get my own bike but I was still under ago so I had to ride round with no tax or insurance. We had no proper clothes and just wore our normal gear.

One day I went with my uncle to Pride and Clarks in Stockwell to get a clutch plate. When we got there they had rows of ex-police bikes for £65. I couldn't believe my eyes — they must have had 150 bikes — maroon Speed Twins with leg shields, fire extinguishers all the gear. I came back and told my mum because I needed her signature on the hire purchase.

When I was 16 I applied for my licence then I insured the bike but we didn't bother about road tax — if you got stopped we gave the usual reply: 'It's in the post!'

In those days we didn't have a lot of money and most of our wages went to keep our bikes up. I was then working for a company called Ross, delivering fish to hospitals, schools, prisons etc. I was getting a bit fed up with going out at four o'clock in the morning although I was finished by half-eleven or 12 o'clock which was nice in the summer.

One of my friends Mick, who had a motorbike and sidecar, told me that his dad had a job going in Walls factory in Atlas Road working in a slaughter house. So I ended up stunning pigs!

After that I went to McVitie & Prices in Waxlow Road where I got the job because of my mechanical knowledge. I was taken on because I was able to repair one of the machines which broke down during my interview!

Left: **'This was the old gatehouse beside the entrance to McVitie's on Waxlow Road where I had a job as a mechanic.** **I used to leave my bike across the road behind this wall** *(right)* **which was open in those days.'**

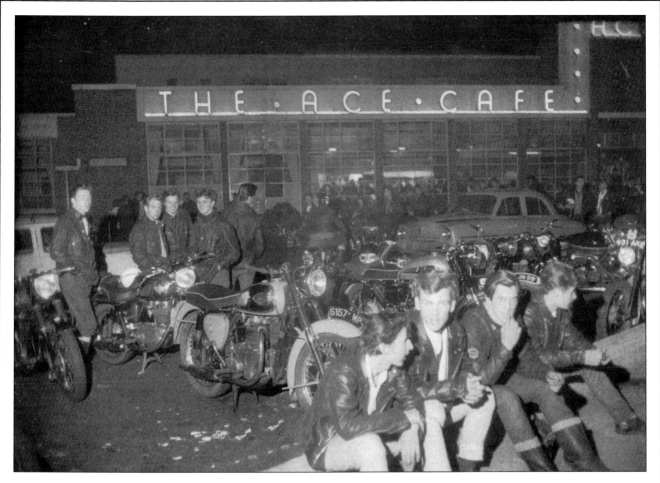

Although I was still knocking about with my mates in Notting Hill, I was out on the bike one day and ended up at the Ace. When I got there I couldn't believe it — there were 200-300 bikes parked outside. I had never seen anything like it before. It was a Thursday night before pay day and nobody had any money.

I pulled up but nobody said anything to me so I started talking to a geezer with a Triumph 110 parked next to me.

His name was Bill and he had a girl with him called Pat. We had some cups of tea and then he asked the time. The girl, who turned out to be his wife, said it was coming up to nine o'clock. She said Bill liked cowboy films and there was one on that night so he said come back and have a cup of tea and watch it. I shot round their house and he said bring the bike down the side and round the back where we could see. They hadn't been

married long and his mother and father-in-law lived upstairs.

We watched the film and that's really how my friendship started. I used to go round his house, and from his house we went to the Ace. I met lads like Kipper, Tiny and Dave and Speedy, Steve, Jenny and Jackie and within a few weeks I was one of the crowd.

∗ ∗ ∗

'This picture of my mate Bill Haddon was taken with his baby daughter Christine outside his house in Bruce Road. At the time Bill was still learning on his BSA and had his L-Plates up.'

London in the 1950s was grimy, grey, dim, quite a dismal place really and winter times were even grimmer with fog and smog from coal fires. We didn't have much money to go anywhere to entertain ourselves but when you went to the Ace, with the name in neon lights, it was like going to America with a jukebox — quite unlike our local caffs. It was all glass fronted and bright with a wall outside where you parked your bike like it was a Wild West saloon.

Sometimes people now ask me: 'What was the Ace really like?' I tell them, if you watch an old cowboy film of Dodge City before Wyatt Earp went in and cleaned it up, that's exactly how the Ace was. The tables and the chairs were bolted to the floor. You went up to the counter just like in a western saloon and you had to use the spoon on a chain to stir your tea!

* * *

In those days you had your ordinary motorcyclist who used his machine for commuting and then you had the enthusiast who liked his machine but would never do anything like we used to do although they would still come to the Ace — like the Triumph Owners Club. They thought we were disgraceful and that we got the name of the bike a bad name.

Although the other popular bikes were Beezas [BSAs] and Nortons, the Triumph had the edge over everybody else, and when Turner produced the Speed Twin in 1938, it was described as possibly the best machine that had ever been produced in this country. And it was.

'Bill was my best mate . . . right from the day I met him at the Ace to the day he was struck down with a heart attack in 1993. I was gutted when he died.'

An afternoon in 1964 . . . one of a marvellous set of photographs taken at the Ace by a north London photographer, Henry Grant.

The nicest part about the Ace was that there never was a local clique there. I had friends in Notting Hill where I lived and mates in Willesden but those at the Ace came from all over. Because they had bikes they were mobile so they arrived from all parts. The other exciting thing about the Ace was that you had several types of people there. First there were your local lads who were not motorcyclists; then you had the last knockings of the Teddy Boys; then there were the lorry drivers, local and long distance; then you had the workers from nearby factories — night workers, day workers, even the people standing waiting at the bus stop. We used to have the women cleaners coming in for an early morning cup of tea. It was just like a little village and it was a real education.

The annexe on the left of the building was the posh part because it had red and white chequered tablecloths and salt and pepper on the table with serviettes. It was separated with a set of doors which gave it a bit of class. You used to get the real working class poor at the Ace but now and again we would get the boys from Harrow School, often in their running kit on a Saturday, who had a Pepsi-Cola through a straw.

We also had the football crowds from Wembley, the dog racers on their nights, the speedway enthusiasts and even coaches with people who had been in the audience in shows at the TV studios up the road. All sorts of people . . . it was wonderful.

And then people started to be flash on their bikes outside. Bill went out there — he really was the business — which is why he got the nick-name 'Mad Bill'. He used to wear a pair of ex-RAF Mk VIII goggles, a leather jacket and gloves but never a helmet. I was then just a spectator and I used to admire him weaving in and out of the traffic.

One night he said: 'Why don't you come out' so I said, 'Alright; I'll have a go.' But to be honest I was absolutely useless. I wasn't used to that sort of riding — aggressive riding. Eventually after knocking around with Bill I got nicked and ended up at the magistrates' court. I was done for £3 but when I told Bill he replied: 'Don't be a silly bastard. You should do what I do. First you stopped. Secondly you've got your right number plate on and thirdly you should just have accelerated and that would have been the end of it.'

At first I used to take my number plates off but in the end we found it was a bit dodgy running around with no plates so we went down Hamrax Motors in Ladbroke Grove — Don and Butch used to run that store — and we used to buy those stick-on number plates. They sold a black background and he would ask what number did you want on it. I'd say 'hang on a minute' and we would go outside the shop. Some old plodder would be going past, so I would say: 'The number is — — — — — —.' And he'd say: 'Your lookin' at that bloke's bike.' I'd reply, 'Never mind about that, just sell us the numbers.' He said: 'I shouldn't be doing this' but I'd tell him: 'OK, I'll just buy the numbers 1 – 10 — you can't stop me.'

With the dodgy plates I could then do anything I liked . . . which I did! And the law used to go mad. because I was immune like the Queen of England!

* * *

Bill's antics soon awarded him the sobriquet 'Mad Bill'. Here he is on the right sporting a single general's star with his Triumph 110. Clive Smith sits on the left. Behind the 'race-track' lies the mountain of Blitz rubble.

I remember once Bill and I were going through Harlesden High Street. We had the dodgy plates on and as we pulled up by the Jubilee clock there was a guy there in a sports car . . . a typical medical student with a flat cap and the old college scarf. It was an MGA and of course when the lights changed Bill and I were off. The driver was chasing us and then we passed these two coppers walking along. They ran out into the road and started throwing things at us — I think they were torches followed by their capes. When we looked round they had stopped the bloke with the MG so we assumed they'd nicked him!

Dirty George would go out in the car park to mend his bike and come in with his hands thick with dirt. He would then sit down and have pie and chips. He never washed and if you saw him the next day he would still have the same shirt on.

* * *

We never used the Lex garage alongside the Ace because we didn't like Regent petrol. We always used Shell from the garage on the corner of Harrow Road. The gas station there now is not the same as it was. If I had trouble with the police, especially when it used to get hot sometimes, I would ride down to that garage and the owner would let me put the bike in the oil store at the side while the law went past. They never thought of coming in the garage. It was a sanctuary for us.

* * *

Above: **Another of Barry's mates, Bob Cannall, enters the Ace car car park at speed — as was the custom. Bob has fitted his 'Ton-ten' with a fly-screen from an Ariel Arrow.** *Right:* **Barry: 'Few of us wore helmets like this lad. I never did until the law changed.'**

I didn't consider myself an experienced rider until I joined what I call 'The Ace Cafe School of Motorcycling'.

There was a bit of hierarchy at the Ace for example if you were a newcomer you wouldn't park facing the wall. When we used to have our burn-ups you would get some of the young lads come up and ask: 'What were you doing past there?' so I would reply: 'Thirty miles an hour!' We were like their heroes and they would buy us cups of tea and even our petrol so we could give entertainment for the lads.

* * *

Mad Bill with his brother Ron on the back of his Thunderbird. They are about to exit the Ace car park to the left. 'We always used to leave the car park this way', says Barry, 'straight on to the Circular . . .

I stuck with the Speed Twin for about a year and then I bought a Thunderbird off of Bill's brother Ron. I then really though I was the business as I was now able to go out and compete with the lads. Once I got the hang of it and there was no stopping me. I behaved exactly like Bill, Kipper and Bob. We were a little set on our own and we didn't pay any attention to the law. We just had it away from them though we may well have been responsible for getting other lads nicked because they just picked on someone else. I don't think the police had ever seen anything like it before.

* * *

. . . but there were a few of the lads who went out the other entrance because they wanted to open up in front of the Ace to show off to those sitting on the wall.'

One chap, new to the Ace, parked on the far side in the lay-by. As he was crossing the road he heard the lovely sound of bikes roaring under the bridges. It really was a beautiful sound. He looked round and saw two bikes approaching. They passed him on the right-hand side but then another bike came hurtling down the road between him and the kerb at 90-100 m.p.h. That was me giving him his introduction to 'Noddy' — Barry Cheese.

* * *

Barry: 'We always used to race on this side of the road because there were less side turnings. I got my nick-name after I filled up my tank at the Shell garage — where the office block now stands in the background — and I forgot to turn the fuel on and ran out right in front of the Ace only to be greeted by a copper on a Velocette known as a 'Noddy' bike: I never lived it down so the lads dubbed me "Noddy"!'

If we were only going to do the short burn-ups — and we never called them that — it was 'Entertainment for the boys'. We would leave the Ace, go under the bridges down to Stonebridge traffic lights and do a U-turn into the south-bound carriageway. We would come back under the bridges and by the time we got back to the Ace we was all into the 90s.

If we were close to each other we would go all the way to Hangar Lane but if one was leading you had proved your point so there was no need.

* * *

'I always took the outside line as we came down under the bridges.'

I was a very slow starter. Whenever they used to turn round at the lights they'd be off before me but then I always tried to time it right to take them opposite the Ace. One day we were all out there — Bill, Blond Bob, Kipper and Clive — and they shut the door on me. So what I did was to go through the opening in the centre and up the wrong side of the road and round back again at the next opening. I came out just in front and when we got back they said to me: 'There's no f*****g point going out with you — you're a lunatic!'

I was very lucky and only had two accidents — not serious. So I must have had a charmed life!

* * *

There was one incident at the Ace which I have always regretted. There was a young fellow there who wasn't quite the full deck of cards. His name was Spot. He never had much money so Len, the bloke behind the counter, used to let him clear the tables. He was a nice harmless chap but we used to take the piss out of him. He rode a pushbike and my mate Bill said one day: 'I'll tell you what. We'll have a laugh with this. Why don't you tow him down the road.'

Well I towed him on his pushbike with a rope on my bike and we must have come past the Ace about 60 m.p.h! Everybody said the funniest thing of all was that there was smoke pouring out of his wheel bearings and brakes and he had a look of sheer horror on his face. I dropped the rope and he came to a standstill under the bridge. At the time it was a laugh but nowadays I consider it would be taking advantage of someone like that.

* * *

Record racing. It *never* happened at the Ace. It was an invention of the BBC in the *Dixon of Dock Green* programme. When I was being interviewed for the film *The Bike's the Star*, they kept on asking me about it. I told them it didn't happen but they said: 'Can't you say it?' I told 'em straight: 'I am not telling lies . . . it never happened.'

The only racing was amongst ourselves. I used to go out with Bill to amuse the lads and we used to do some really stupid things. Sometimes I would sit round the other way on his pillion seat and wave to the police as we went past which was like having a nodding dog in the back of a car!

Even the law had to laugh but I remember one copper coming in one day and saying to me: 'I'll get you, you bastard!' I said: 'What?' 'He said: 'That was you on that bike!' 'No, not me! Not f*****g much it wasn't!'

* * *

'This was our race-track as we neared the final bridges before the Ace.'

Left: **Nice shot of Johnny who has just passed Barry's escape route down Iveagh Avenue.** *Above:* **With the reconstruction of this section of the North Circular in the mid-1990s, the road was sealed off but the bus stop remains.**

If we were being chased we used to turn left into Iveagh Avenue a few hundred yards beyond the Ace. Down the side behind the factory was a little alleyway and just out the back of it was a little courtyard and a car park. If the law was chasing us we would do a quick left up there; go down this alley and cut the engine. They had all this junk where we used to hide as we heard the bells on the police cars or bikes going by. We'd sit down there having a fag while it all cooled down.

Barry: 'We used to turn up here and go down beside the factory until the coppers went past'.

Night falls at the Ace . . . waiting for the action to begin . . . then and now.

I remember once pulling up at a set of lights when this copper came up beside me. I was on a dodgy plate but I thought if he doesn't say nothing, I won't do anything. But all of a sudden there were two of them — they usually rode in pairs — and he said to me: 'Pull over!' I never wore a helmet but these coppers were all done up on their Speed Twins with all the gear and gauntlets. I replied: 'Alright. When the lights change I'll pull round the corner.'

So of course when the lights changed, I pulled round the corner . . . but I didn't stop. And that was the end of it — I never saw them again!

*　*　*

One night Bill and I were out there on our own. We were being bloody stupid really, giving it the full works up and down. On the way back under the bridges, there was a lorry parked on the lay-by opposite. As we were coming up I saw the driver run quickly over the road but his mate was dawdling across, probably thinking he would make us slow down. Well I went one side of him and Bill the other — whoof — just like that! All the lads said he just froze in his tracks.

∗ ∗ ∗

I never had to worry about the law knocking on the door — only once when I borrowed someone's bike and his girlfriend grassed me up. Then I got nicked for everything. My mum came to court and the magistrate was quite good because he asked the Clerk of the Court if there was any way of taking my motorbike licence away and leaving my car licence because of my work. But the Clerk told him: 'No. If you take it, you've got to take it all.' So when he heard that, the magistrate said he wouldn't take my licence away. The law was in court and they just held their heads in their hands. But I was fined £40 which was a hell of a lot in those days.

∗ ∗ ∗

Len Hopkins was the main manager in the Golden Years. I was in the car park one day with a few of the lads but it was quiet so Bill said: 'Cor! We need some action and I need a cup of tea.' So I said to him: 'Open the doors!' I started my bike up, rode up into the cafe and up to the counter. I had to go down the centre because of the tables and as I pulled up I said: 'Four teas please.' And Len replied: 'No, three! You're barred!'

∗ ∗ ∗

The day the jukebox (a Seeburg AY with 160 selections manufactured in 1961) went for a ride — courtesy of Barry and Mad Bill! Wally Osborne in the turned-up jeans lounges beside the entrance while Blond Bob, Jimmy and Joan sit at the 'top table'.

We was all in the car park one night — there wasn't a lot going on — and this bloke came in with this lorry, a flatback lorry. It was obvious that he had just dropped his load at one of the factories in Park Royal and come in to get his meal — that's what they used to do — before returning up north.

We noticed that he had this rope on his motor so I said to Bill we'll have a laugh here and pull that jukebox out. So we hooked the rope on the back of his lorry and waited until the record finished. We then unplugged the jukebox, pulled it out and put the rope round it. When the bloke started moving he didn't even know he was towing a jukebox! Len ran out after the lorry shouting at him to stop. We killed ourselves laughing. After that Len put an armoured cage around it to stop it happening again.

∗ ∗ ∗

Thunderbird in part exchange and my mum signed the HP. When I got the Bonneville I went straight down to Bob's at Witton. Off came the handlebars and we added an Ariel flyscreen so mine was exactly like his.

* * *

One day I was on the way down to the Ace from my house in Mortimer Road and as I turned left off the Harrow Road onto the Circular, two coppers on motorbikes were sitting just around the corner. I had come round the corner a bit hairy so I thought its too late now — in for a penny in for a pound. So I thought I might as well just carry on.

Sure enough they came after me, and were behind me so I thought, well I'm on dodgy number plates and the Ace will be packed. I opened up under the bridges and these two opened up as well. By the time we got to the Ace all the lads were standing on the wall

Barry with his new Bonneville outside Bill's house in Craven Park. The number plate in this picture — somewhat appropriate in view of Barry's antics — is actually the genuine one!

Blond Bob came down the Ace one day in 1961 with his brand new Bonneville. He said: 'What do you think of it?' I replied: 'Well, let me have a ride on it.' He agreed but added: 'OK, but just take care with it.' Which I did. It was really nice with twin carbs and I thought I've got to have one of these. So I went over to Harwoods at Richmond. He said he hadn't got one at the moment but that there was one coming although he had a lot of people wanting it. Bob put in a good word for me so they took my

Forty years later . . . a nostalgic return visit to Bruce Road.

'If we were being chased, once we turned into Iveagh Avenue we sometimes kept going to Bill's house. We would turn left into Abbey Road and follow the road round into Acton Lane by the hospital [Central Middlesex]. We then did an immediate left after Harlesden Station into Mordaunt, a right into Shrewsbury and right again into Knatchbull with a quick right and left at the end into Bruce Road. Bill's sideway has changed since those days but this is where we hid the bikes until the coast was clear.'

cheering so I thought to myself I'm not just going to continue up the road. It was all bravado in those days — even I've got to admit we were flash. So when I reached the Ace, I decided to act as if I was going to turn right into the car park. The coppers were right behind me but instead of turning into the car park I just turned round and went down the Ace side of the Circular to the next intersection and round again.

So there we were going round and round with all the lads cheering but after a couple of times I thought they are going to suss this out and one of them is going to stay back and one follow me. So on the second circuit I just opened up and f***ed off and left them standing there. They chased me up the road but I did a quick left down Iveagh Avenue round the back doubles, through the back of Harlesden and Craven Park to Bruce Road and up to Bill's house. Bill's side entrance was always left unlocked for us so we used to wheel our bikes through and shut the door.

Sometimes Bill would be down the Ace but his wife Pat would be sitting at home as she had the baby then watching the telly. So I used to knock on the windows and she would open the door and let me in. And I would then phone down to the Ace and ask for Bill to tell him that I was round his house. He'd say: 'No, don't come back, they're still waiting here for you.' And that's how we used to do it.

* * *

Once I got the Bonneville, that's when things really started. We used to take diabolical liberties out there although we never ventured far along the North Circular and the fancy stuff was really all confined to the Ace Cafe area.

I had one incident near the Book Centre by the Iron Bridge with two coppers and Irish Dick. I was down the Ace one Saturday afternoon and the only other person in there was Irish Dick who had a Road Rocket. He said: 'Do you fancy a ride down to the Bee?' I said: 'Yeah alright then,' so we shot down the Busy Bee at Watford — a run of about 20-25 minutes.

Our route to the Busy Bee was to go up the Circular past the Iron Bridge and turn left into Village Way just before the Neasden crossroads. At the end we turned right down Quainton Street and then left into Blackbird Hill. We went straight up Salmon Street, across the junction into Fryant Way and then across Kingsbury Road to Honeypot Lane. We then rode up to Marsh Lane, across the London Road at Stanmore into Dennis Lane and turned right at the T-junction with Wood Lane. We then came to the T on Brookley Hill where we turned left to the Watford bypass and the Bee was a couple of miles up the road just past The Spiders Web.

On the way back we used to come up Neasden Lane to the traffic lights and turn right on to the North Circular. Coming down to the bridge I was being a bit flash on the outside and he was on the inside. We came over the Iron Bridge with the Book Centre on our left and then stopped at the set of traffic lights with the garage on the corner of Brentfield Road.

Just before we got there, Dick called over: 'Be careful! There's the Old Bill behind us.' I looked round but it was just a van so I took no notice. With that, two motorcycle coppers shot between us. The lights were red and there was a stationary car there in the middle of the road. One of the coppers said to me: 'When the lights change you pair of c***s, pull over! I'm booking the f*****g pair of you!'

Speed-cops used to wear those big gauntlets at the time so I tapped on his hand: 'Well, here's one c**t you ain't bookin! Ta ta!' And with that I was off. Gone. Well, I didn't care because I was on dodgy plates.

'This is where I took off from when the motorbike coppers ordered me to pull over. I had come down the southbound carriageway from Neasden and was stationary in the outside lane with a car in between me and Irish Dick.'

Later Dick told me what then took place. He said: 'When you left the scene you were in second gear and off up the road before the copper realised what had happened.' Dick explained that he was laughing so much and became so hysterical that he dropped his bike which fell onto the car. The other copper set off after me but came back about 10 minutes later. They took Dick up the Nick and when they got up there, they said: 'Look. We're not interested in you. Just give us the name of that guy and you are free to go.' Dick said: 'I've never seen him in my life before. I've just been up Slocombes to get some parts when I saw this bloke coming down.'

They had him up the Nick for 3½ hours and in the end they let him go. He only knew me as 'Noddy' but was aware of where Mad Bill lived so he shot round there and left a message for me to keep clear. I had to stay away from the cafe as the police started sitting there, drinking tea, waiting for me. However, after about two weeks it fizzled out and we were back to our old tricks again.

* * *

'He was going at it tight but all the others were open so they could see further round the bend. Tiny was on top of the car when he hit it. Dave fell on the kerb which smashed all his right-hand ribs in. Tiny went straight across the road when he lost control and hit the nearside kerb. He went over the handlebars and got hit by his own bike. The clutch lever went into his spleen or something."' Tiny (Robert Griffiths) lived in the Harrow Road and Dave Lambert, the pillion passenger, in Marley Close, Greenford. Both were fatally injured at the scene: Tiny with a fractured spine and Dave having ruptured his aorta. They were rushed to Willesden General Hospital in Harlesden Road but to no avail. It was Saturday November 10, 1960 — the day before Remembrance Sunday. They had crashed almost at the same spot where Bobby Owen (see page 65) had come to grief three years previously (see also page 84).

'It was just opposite here, outside the Pantiles (above) which is now a McDonalds, that Tiny and Dave were killed. I was at the Ace at the time but I'll always remember it as the jukebox was playing *Only the Lonely* when they came and told us. When I got there the bike was all smashed up just here (right). Later my mate "Wig" [Tony Evans] told me what happened. He said that Tiny, who was a great big bloke, and Dave told him they were going to the Cherie — a coffee bar in Borehamwood High Street. Wiggy had agreed to give a girl a lift but had to pull into the Shell garage first for petrol. "In the meantime," Wiggy explained, "this lot has gone flying up there like lunatics at 80 or 90. I was doing about 70 trying to catch them up when I saw a load of brake lights coming on. Basically what happened was that a car came out of the side road and stuck his nose through the central reservation. Tiny was right on the centre of the road.

Johnny and Jimmy pass the lay-by — scene of one of Noddy's boldest exploits. On this occasion Mad Bill *(right)* **was the instigator!**

Another time a huge transformer was being moved towards Hangar Lane on a massive two-trailer rig which had to have a police escort. There were six coppers on motorbikes with flashing blue lights. They weren't local speed cops, but traffic unit used for escort They pulled into the lay-by and walked over to get refreshment.

We were all in the car park and the law had all come over leaving their Speed Twins lined up on the other side of the road. The coppers were all standing at the counter to get their cups of tea so Bill said to me: 'Look at those bikes. I would love to have a go on one of them.' So he said to me: 'Why don't you have a go and see how fast they can do?' He wasn't stupid because he said: 'I'll ride my bike and you ride one of theirs!'

The lay-by was lost when the new dual carriageway was built to avoid the constriction caused by the old railway bridges.

'This was the key I used to start the police bike.'

'I rode up to the junction with the Harrow Road and into the Shell garage which used to be on this corner'.

In those days it only needed a simple spade key to start a bike so I went over round the back of the lorry while the lads kept watch on the police. I decided to take the one at the back but I first looked in the tank. They must have just refuelled because it was full so I put the key in, started her up. I then thought I might as well give the boys the full works so I put the blue lights on as well!

So with all the lads pissing themselves with laughter, and with the coppers unaware of what was going on, Bill and I went up and down the road but then they spotted the flashing lights. When they came running out me and Bill lit off towards Neasden. The lads told me afterwards that two of them ran to their bikes and set off after me. We knew they would come after us so when we reached the Shell garage, I pulled in, put the bike on its stand, and jumped on the back of Bill's bike and we were away.

When the law arrived the chap serving petrol said that two blokes had left on a bike. As the police bikes were only single-seaters, one had to stay with the bike until the rider had walked down from the Ace. Probably out of embarrassment, it was never reported and they never came after us.

✳ ✳ ✳

'I left the bike here and rode off with Bill on the back of his Bonne.'

The gang on 'the Wall'. Mad Bill is third from the left and sixth is Bob Cannall.

The Wall 40 years on. The railings were added after 1969 when the cafe closed and was later converted into a tyre-fitting centre.

Once we had done one bit of bravado, we went on to do more. I remember once when Bob came down to show us his new Triumph Norton in full racing trim. As it had no number plates and a full megaphone exhaust, he brought it down in the van to show the lads. Anyway he started it up — it was a right noisy beast but, by God, it was quick. I said: 'Come on let me have a go on it,' so I went out on it, winding it up on towards Harrow and back under the bridges. As I came back these two speed-cops were coming down the other way. By the time they had turned round, I had done a U-turn and was on my way back. There we were, up and down, me hoping there was enough petrol in it to carry on so I had it away to Bill's house. I went in and phoned the Ace to ask Bill to tell Bob the bike was OK at his house and to bring the van to pick it up.

∗ ∗ ∗

Back in those days there used to be an RAC caravan sitting in the Ace car park manned by a resident patrolman who also sold memberships in the summer. What we used to do to boost his trade was to park our bikes all round any car that pulled in and tell the driver: 'Look, you should join the RAC because you never know what might happen to your car. The wing mirror might fall off . . . all sorts of things!'

∗ ∗ ∗

Sometimes I would go down with Bill in his Commer van but the boys would still want 'entertainment' so we would borrow bikes. If we said we didn't have our bikes, people would say 'well you can borrow ours' but I used to tell them 'to protect you we'll take the number plates off.'

∗ ∗ ∗

Barry: 'The local old Bill used to come down when their canteen closed to buy pies to take back. One day this chap came in on a Noddy bike, left it by the entrance, and some of the lads — I know their names but they will remain anonymous — picked it up and threw it in the river at the back.'

Waiting for the burn-ups . . . then and now. Friday and Saturday nights especially would see up to 200 bikes massed on the forecourt.

All the lads were down there watching on the wall. It was pretty neck and neck going up so I thought Bollocks! I'm going to give it the full f***ing works.

As we came down to the Ace — we must have been doing 90-95 — I'm on the outside and he's on the inside. Then, all of a sudden, this f***ing van pulled out. I always remember it was a 100E Ford. As it pulled out I saw his brake lights go on. It was a split-second decision so instead of braking I opened up and went round him but Tony hit the van — Bang! We thought he was a goner and for three days he was in intensive care.

* * *

We used to do some terrible things. There was one night — I think it was 1963 when Tony River came down to the Ace with a brand new unit-construction Bonneville. He was a good rider and was quick and he wanted someone to go out with him but I said I hadn't got my Bonnie any more. But old Kipper said: 'Oh, I'll get you a Bonneville' . . . and they did — a '61 — so I went out there with him.

We did a left out of the Ace and down the road to the traffic lights, did the usual U-ey and back up again. It was more a neck and neck race — the new Bonnie against the old Bonnie — and it was good. I was enjoying the competition as it was very, very tight.

Anyway, when we got up to the top he said: 'Fancy another run back?' 'Well', I said, 'we don't normally race down this side because of the side turnings.' But he insisted: 'Oh come on'. So I replied: 'All right if you want to.'

Noddy caught at last! Barry stands where he was collared by the law on the evening of February 10, 1961 — we will see more of this police operation to curb the excesses at the Ace later.

On our nostalgic tour around Willesden, Barry revisited Harlesden police station on the corner of Craven Park, still the same as it was 40 years ago.

One day in February 1961 I pulled in on my bike and there was a geezer standing at the bus stop. Quite respectable with a bowler hat in his hand with his briefcase. He had just commented: 'That's a nice machine' before police vans were coming in. A copper came up and said: 'You're nicked!' and turning to the chap at the bus stop: 'So are you,' and they grabbed him as well.

Anyway, when we got up the Harlesden Nick we spent two or three hours in the cells. They charged us two together with insulting behaviour and they said we were throwing cups which was a load of bollocks because I said to the copper: 'If that was going on, as you say it was, the first sign we'd have seen of you and we'd have f***ed off.' I said: 'The reason we didn't is that it didn't happen did it? And I know why you came down because you have had a directive from the f***ing Home Office because an arsehole journalist wrote about this place and dicing with death. The Home Office has leaned on your guvnor and he's come down on you to send a load of young rookies in a van to trump up charges against us.'

Anyway the next thing I knew they had asked the other guy his name and he showed them a card. The sergeant then said to me: 'Come here a minute you!' so I went over and he said: 'Right you two, f**k off.' It turned out that the other chap was a solicitor who had just visited a local company. So that's how me and him walked out of the Nick and all the rest got done.

* * *

BLOND BOB

We all lined ourselves up — there was Mad Billy, Blond Bob and myself — and we were all going to go to the Odeon in Craven Park with some birds. We met at the Ace but Bob never turned up — we found later that he had gone to the Dugout instead. We were in Bill's van with the three girls. Well after the film we couldn't get anywhere with the girls so we dropped them off and went to Bill's in Bruce Road to get our bikes. When we got to the Ace we were greeted with the news: 'Have you heard about Bob?' 'What do you mean?' 'He has been involved in a serious accident at Hendon Way.'

So Bill and I went straight to the local hospital at Park Royal only to find that Bob had been taken instead to the Royal Orthopaedic at Stanmore but we couldn't see him as they were operating. When we were finally able to see him a couple of days later he was pretty cheerful but when we came out of his room I commented to Bill about the smell. I asked the nurse and she said he had gangrene and would have to lose his arm although they hadn't told him and didn't know how to. The doctor was called and I asked him if he would like me to give him the bad news. So Bill and I went back in and sat on Bob's bed.

I said: 'Listen, let me tell you something, but before I tell you, first of all we will always be yer mates and we ain't going to abandon you. But because of the accident you know you are going to lose your arm because they can't do anything for you and it's gangrenious. You can smell it can't you?'

Bob agreed and said he already had an idea about it. I told him that we would still be mates and they do wonderful things these days and that he might be back on a bike. 'If not,' I said, 'you'll be on the back of one of ours.'

Nick (left) makes a point to Blond Bob in the doorway of the Ace.

Bill and I went to pick up his bike — a Bonneville — which had been left in a service station and I put it in my garage. His dad came round and I said we would take it to Harwoods at Richmond to get it repaired but it was then sold.

Fortunately for Bob he could drive so he had a false arm fitted and got a Mk I Zephyr off of Ray. I fitted a necking knob on the steering wheel and he was OK. I fixed him a job with a photographic company driving round to chemists shops but after that I didn't see him for some time. I met him later outside Bill's house. He said he was fed up and told me that he couldn't do the things he wanted to do. Finally, he admitted: 'I really don't think its all worth it.'

I said to him: 'You're not going to do anything silly are you? Don't because you have still got all your mates. You are welcome to come round — come round to dinner . . . which he did.'

He then found a girl but the next I heard he was back on his own. Bill saw him a couple of times and I saw him once when I repaired the dynamo on his car. I then lost contact and never saw him again. Years later I was told that he had taken his own life which was such a sad end to one of my close mates and one of the real characters at the Ace. I was so choked at what had happened that I used to tell people that he had lost his life at Hendon . . . which in a way he had.

Left: **Blond Bob (Robert Wafer) after the accident at Hendon in which he lost his right arm, pictured with Mad Bill and baby Christine.** *Above:* **A sad day for Barry on the same spot in Bruce Road today. Two of his best mates now departed . . . but not forgotten.**

Few of the old cafes frequented by the 'coffee-bar cowboys' in north London in the late 1950s-early 1960s survived. The Ace closed in 1969; the Busy Bee was demolished the same year; Ted's Transport at Charlie Brown's roundabout on the Southend Road was knocked down in 1975 and the Cherie in Borehamwood sold up and was converted into a formal restaurant.

One of the other cafes we used to ride to was the Dugout which was down a little mews near the Golders Green station. The guy who used to run it was named Ramsey. If we were going to the Dugout, we'd go up the North Circular to Hendon Way — then there was no roundabout or flyover. We used to turn right into Hendon Way and then left into Wayside and along the Vale to Finchley Road.

* * *

Only the Dugout, close by Golders Green Station, has stood the test of time and Barry called in after our tour for a welcome cuppa.

Barry had his first leather jacket stolen and has more recently given his second away as an encouragement to a young lad. But he still has his gloves and scarf . . .

It started to happen about 1963 — drugs — which was the reason why most of us pulled out of the Ace. We tolerated it for a bit but then it got out of hand. In the end, the addicts took it over and the decent people who used to go there decided to give it a miss. After '65 it disintegrated and I never went down there any more after 1966.

* * *

Then I had Triumphs — I was a Triumph man. I still ride on a regular basis but now my preferred hack which I use most of all is my little Honda 50. Everybody laughs at me but it keeps me mobile . . . it keeps me on the road . . . and I don't lose my streetwise road sense. And I've still got a BSA Rocket Gold Star in the back of the garage . . . so you never know when Noddy might ride again one day!

BARRY CHEESE, 2002

. . . and a beautifully restored Gold Star!

The Golden Years

Petrol rationing was introduced in September 1939 and there were limited supplies for civilian motoring only until March 1942. The post-war petrol allowance was 180 miles per month . . . that is until that glorious day in 1950!

Undeterred by the price hike in last month's budget, Britain's army of car owners hit the road — and the country's forecourts — today to celebrate the start of the Whitsun holiday and the end of petrol rationing. Drivers at some garages were reportedly tearing up ration books and dancing around their cars. Officials of the Automobile Association called the traffic volume 'an all-time record' as 10 years of restrictions were lifted.

Ten-mile-long streams of cars were reported heading for London, while a mini-heatwave in the south helped create a massive exodus to coast resorts. Shares in hotel and leisure companies shot up in the Stock Exchange and civic leaders in holiday destinations predicted a boom to their towns after years of lean pickings.

Press report, May 30, 1950

On July 4, 1947 — US Independence Day — an American Motorcyclists Association race competition in Hollister, California, got completely out of hand when drunken riders ranged through the town, racing and jumping red lights. Frank Rooney wrote up the story in *Harper's Magazine* in 1951 and his novel *The Cyclist's Raid* inspired Laslo Benedek's film *The Wild One* released in 1954. This was initially banned in Britain because there was no retribution shown in the film for the motorcycle gang, led by Marlon Brando, which terrorised a small town. The image created by Brando of a black leather jacket and turned-up jeans over black boots did much to influence post-war 'teenagers' who aspired to associate themselves with the freedom offered by motorcycling. At the beginning of the 1950s, America had just over 50 million vehicles on the road compared to Britain's 4½ million. That year, save for pedestrians of whom 2,251 were killed, motorcyclists topped the accident list with 1,129 deaths compared with 827 on four wheels and 805 on pedal cycles. (The comparative UK figures today (2000) are 857 pedestrians, 127 pedal cycles, 605 motorcyclists and 1,820 other road users. Motorcycle deaths were at an all-time high in 1960 at 1,743.

There are two gleams of hope in the road casualty figures for 1954. The first is that the increase of 11,511 in casualties compared with 1953 occurred entirely among adult road users. The number of child deaths fell by 135 to 662 and there was also a slight decrease in the number of children seriously injured. This is some proof that the road safety instruction given by the Police and others to school children is bearing fruit, and the saving of 135 young lives is something which all engaged in road safety propaganda can regard with sober pride. Casualties in all road accidents in 1954 numbered 238,281, an increase of 11,511 on the figures for 1953. Deaths numbered 5,010, a decrease of 80; serious injuries 57,201, an increase of 679; and slight injuries 176,070, an increase of 10,912. This sombre record is the price the country has to pay for the failure of successive Governments to face up to the problem of road traffic and to make provision for the fivefold increase in the number of motor vehicles during the past thirty years.

The Police Review, March 11, 1955

Britain is set to enter the jukebox age. Recently freed from restrictive controls, the industry manufacturing these public record players is poised to emulate its success in America, where the number of boxes in operation is said to number half a million — one for every 300 of the population!

On a visit to Britain, John Haddock, owner of the leading US manufacturer AMI, said an ideal location for jukeboxes would be the coffee houses which have become a London institution and are rapidly spreading to the provinces. 'In the States', he points out, 'music is usually associated with refreshment'.

So the British should look out for records with their coffee. If the jukebox makers have a say in the matter, silent refreshment is on its way out!

Press report, February 1955

With the plethora of music-making machinery now available, and piped music everywhere, it is difficult for the younger generation today to understand the excitement of being able to play a popular record at will from a jukebox. The machine in this picture was state-of-the-art in 1959-60 — the first stereo Wurlitzer in a roadside cafe-cum-coffee bar.

According to Vic Bettencourt, the first Hell's Angels' motorcycle club was formed soon after the Hollister incident in Berdoo by an offshoot from a renegade group called the Pissed off Bastards of Fontana, California. 'Motorcycles became the thing to ride in California after World War II,' says Ralph 'Sonny' Barger, one of the leading lights. 'A lot of the GIs coming home from the Pacific who didn't want to return to some boring life in Indiana or Kentucky chose to stick around California. A motorcycle was a cheap mode of transportation, kind of dangerous and perfect for racing and hanging out. Plus they could ride together, just like they were back in the sevice again. California became the center of motorcycle culture, and for years there were more motorcycles registered there than in all the other states combined. I met Vic in the late summer of 1957 and it set my mind to thinking about what was needed for our Oakland Chapter and in 1958 I took over as president.'

THE REAL STORY BEHIND THE...
HELL'S ANGELS
AND OTHER 'OUTLAW' MOTORCYCLE GROUPS
BY BOB GRANT
AN INTIMATE PHOTO STORY OF THEIR EVERY ACT—FROM SMOKING 'POT' TO LOVE MAKING—THEIR WOMEN • THEIR BIKES • THEIR DRUNKEN ORGIES • THEIR KIDS

This month's most unusual US chart entry is *Black Denim Trousers and motorcycle Boots*, recorded by Capitol Records group The Cheers. The idea came from Marlon Brando's *The Wild One* — banned in Britain after the censors described it as 'a screen essay in violence and brutality'.

Meanwhile, we learn of the death of James Dean, who had been widely tipped as 'the new Brando'. Dean (24) whose first major film *East of Eden* opens in London this month, died at the wheel of his Porsche sports car on September 30.

It is a gruesome coincidence that, like the motorcycle hero of The Cheers' record (cut weeks earlier), he was killed on Highway 101 in California. Two more Dean movies are in the can, awaiting release: *Rebel Without a Cause* and *Giant*.

The role of Rocky Grazziano in *Somebody Up There Likes Me*, which Dean was to play, has now been assigned to screen newcomer Paul Newman.

Press report, October 1955

BLACK DENIM TROUSERS AND MOTORCYCLE BOOTS

He wore black denim trousers and motorcycle boots,
And a black leather jacket with an eagle on the back,
He had a hopped-up 'cicle that took off like a gun,
That fool was the terror of Highway 101.

Well, he never washed his face and he never combed his hair.
He had axle grease imbedded underneath his fingernails.
On the muscle of his arm was a red tattoo,
A picture of a heart saying 'Mother, I love you'.

He had a pretty girlfriend by the name of Mary Lou,
But he treated her just like he treated all the rest.
And everybody pitied her and everybody knew,
He loved that doggone motorcycle best.

He wore black denim trousers and motorcycle boots,
And a black leather jacket with an eagle on the back.
He had a hopped-up 'cicle that took off like a gun,
That fool was the terror of Highway 101.

Mary Lou, poor girl, she pleaded and she begged him not
*   to leave,*
She said 'I've got a feeling if you ride tonight I'll grieve'.
But her tears were shed in vain and her every word was lost,
In the rumble of an engine and the smoke from his exhaust:

'Then he took off like the Devil and there was fire in his
eyes! He said: "I'll go a thousand miles before the sun can
rise." But he hit a screamin' diesel that was California-
bound.'

And when they cleared the wreckage, all they found
Was his black denim trousers and motorcycle boots,
And a black leather jacket with an eagle on the back.
But they couldn't find the 'cicle that took off like a gun,
And they never found the terror of Highway 1-oh-1.

WORDS AND MUSIC ©
JERRY LEIBER AND MIKE STOLLER

'I went to the Wembley garage (see page 73) in 1952,' recalls ex-PC916 John Gillett, 'and stayed until 1959 when I became a driving instructor at Hendon Police Driving School. We had over 80 drivers at Wembley split into shifts, either 7 a.m. to 3 p.m.; 3 p.m. to 11 p.m. or 8 a.m. to 4 p.m. and 4 p.m. to midnight. We covered three police divisions, two inner and one outer, which meant that we were patrolling a huge area from Oxford Circus to Denham and Hackney to Bushey. There were a number of traffic accident cars — over the years Wolseley 18/85s, 6/80s, 6/99s, 6/110s — equipped with R/T to New Scotland Yard, and the driver and radio operator would change roles half way through the shift. We rode Triumph Speed-Twins, 5Ts and 6Ts (Thunderbirds), each bike being maintained in tip-top condition and they had complete overhauls every 6,000 miles. On June 19, 1959, I had a call over the wireless to proceed to an RTA [Road Traffic Accident] near the Ace Cafe at Stonebridge Park. The picture shows the scene that confronted me when I reached the spot.

'The fire appliance — a Dennis F12 from the Middlesex County Fire Brigade at Stonebridge Park — had been proceeding westwards on an emergency to Alperton and was turning right to go up Heather Park Drive. The lorry was coming in the opposite direction carrying 12-tons of windscreens for delivery to the Triplex factory. Presuming that the lorry would stop to let it through, the fire engine turned across the road and they both met in the middle of the carriageway. The impact turned the engine through 180 degrees and threw the driver, Fireman Joseph Clark, through the windscreen. The driverless fire engine continued to move forward under its own power only to run over the unconscious fireman lying in the road, killing him.'

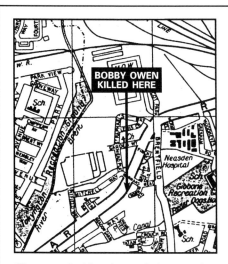

'The worst incident I attended concerning the Ace boys was the fatal accident of Bobby Owen on October 18, 1957. That evening I was parked in the entrance to Stonebridge Park LT Station *(above right)* from where I could hear the motorcycles start up. Some bikes tore up the road past me but the automatic traffic signals were against me at the Harrow Road junction which was much too dangerous for me to cross on red. As I waited for the lights to change, a motorist on the far carriageway stopped and came running over, heading for the telephone box on the corner. He saw me and said he wanted to report a serious accident on the first left-hand bend *(right)* down the road towards Neasden where a motorbike was on fire with the rider sprawled in the road. I asked him to call the ambulance and fire brigade before setting off. When I reached the scene of the accident it was obvious that nothing could be done for the rider who was most seriously injured and already dead. A passing doctor confirmed this for me. It appeared that through excessive speed he had lost control on the bend and his bike had ridden like a wall of death up the wire netting separating the carriageways before he collided with a concrete lamp standard. The riders that he had probably been racing against were returning down the other side but did not stop.'

'I let it be known at the Ace Cafe that I wanted to talk to them and a few days later I received a message over the radio that some had turned up voluntarily at Harlesden police station where I took statements from them. They were from Borehamwood and they later attended the Coroner's hearing on October 29 to give evidence of events before the accident. It came out that Bobby's girlfriend would not go with him on the back of his bike as she said it was too dangerous and had instead agreed to return later on a friend's bike. A report was submitted to our legal branch although they were reluctant to prosecute them for racing on the highway through lack of hard evidence.'

On Monday the number of lightweight motorcycles used for beat patrol in the outer Divisions of the Metropolitan Police was increased by ninety. In a statement to the Press, the Commissioner emphasised that the members of the Force patrolling on these motorcycles may be stopped and called upon by the public for any normal purpose for which a Police officer may be required.

The Police Review, October 11, 1957

January has proved a tragic month on local roads, with five fatal accidents in the Observer area during the first two weeks of the month. Four of these were in Harrow — exactly half the total number of fatal street accidents in Harrow for the whole of last year — and one in Wembley, where last year's fatal accidents totalled ten. One was a motorcyclist, Mr. William Houghton, aged 23, of 77 Cavendish Avenue, Sudbury Hill, who was involved in an accident in Harrow Road, Sudbury, on January 1.

Harrow Observer, January 16, 1958

Witnesses at Hendon Coroner's Court on Monday told of an accident on New Year's Day which led to the death of a 23-year-old motorcyclist, Mr. William Houghton of 77 Cavendish Avenue, Sudbury Hill, and to injuries to his brother, Michael.

The Observer and Gazette,
February 6, 1958

Harrow's 'black' month on the roads ended with another tragic death last week. This latest victim was 18-year-old Trevor Allan Evans, of 39 Kings Road, South Harrow, who was killed when the motorcycle he was riding was in collision with a coal lorry in Chicheley Road, Cricklewood. Mr. Evans was taken to Willesden General Hospital but found to be dead on arrival.

Harrow Observer, February 6, 1958

Six people were killed on local roads in January. Arguments are often put forward that it is the entire responsibility of drivers and riders to avoid pedestrians on the road. If that were really the case it would be the entire responsibility of pedestrians to avoid vehicles on the pavement.

The responsibility for avoiding accidents

As accidents on motorcycles mounted: 1,175 in 1952; 1,237 in 1953; 1,352 two years later; 1,425 in 1957 and 1,680 in 1969, newspapers were full of reports of deaths and injuries. This incident occurred on June 30, 1956 — location not stated but it was obviously in the London area in view of the LCC ambulance attending the scene.

rests on everyone. That you have not been involved in an accident does not mean you may have achieved perfection in the use of the roads. We all have our faults which, if not corrected, sooner or later lead to an 'accident.'

As a driver, do you never go a little over the speed limit, always give way to 'the other fellow,' give good signals in time, park considerately and take extra care at crossroads? When walking do you always stop first and look before crossing, and if there is a crossing use it; do you never say, 'He can pull up,' when perhaps he might not have seen you? Motorcycling and cycling call for skill, but ice and greasy surfaces need more than skill. Do you never, when motorcycling cut a corner, or when cycling ride two, or even three, abreast, and always look round first to see if it is clear to pull out?

If you are starting to motorcycle, have just bought a car, junior is not too safe on his bicycle, or your dog just will not do exactly what you want why not write to the local council? They have put into operation many schemes to help reduce accidents.

Councillor E. S. W. Atherton,
Harrow Road Safety Council, February 6, 1958

Gordon Hepburn, aged 19, of 125 Weald Lane, Harrow Weald, died on Tuesday night in Kingston Hospital from injuries received when a motorcycle on which he was riding pillion crashed into a roundabout in Hampton Court Way, Thames Ditton. The driver Peter Hammond, aged 21, is in hospital with head injuries.

Harrow Observer, March 6, 1958

A 70 m.p.h.. motorcycle chase along Eastcote Lane, South Harrow, on February 28, had a sequel at Harrow Court on Friday, when Elwyn John Hester, of Wickham Road, Wealdstone, was fined £5 for speeding and disqualified for two years for speeding dangerously, and was ordered to pay 10s 6d costs. He pleaded guilty to the first offence and not guilty to the second.

Police Constable C. Williams said that he was on his motorcycle in Field End Road, Ruislip, on February 28, when he saw Hester riding along Victoria Road towards Eastcote Lane at a very high speed. When he reached the roundabout, Hester was 200 yards ahead and accelerating. He chased him along Eastcote Road at speeds ranging between 68 and 70 m.p.h., until they were forced to stop at the traffic lights at Alexandra Avenue.

PC Williams continued that on the way Hester had passed four cars, and in doing so had forced three cars approaching in the opposite direction to hug the pavement.

On oath, Hester claimed that he had perfect control of his machine, and that the constable 'saw a lot' for the speed at which they were travelling.

Replying to questions, he said at that speed it would have taken him 100 yards to pull up.

It was stated that he had been fined in November of last year at Harrow Court for speeding.

Observer Gazette, May 1, 1958

A young Harlesden man gave evidence in Willesden Court on Thursday that after seeing a car crash into a lamp standard opposite the Ace Cafe, North Circular Road, Stonebridge, he went across to it and, in the front seat, saw the driver, a girl and another man unconscious. In the back lay a woman, with a girl sitting on top of her. Later, he saw another man coming from the back of the car.

Mr. Arthur James Reuter, a TV engineer, of Kenilworth Court, Curzon Crescent, gave evidence that on May 18 he was driving home from Heston in his black Standard car, when it broke down. He started to tow the car with his firm's A30 van, his brother-in-law, Mr. Gordon Pearce, driving the towed car.

At about 11.55 p.m. they were approaching the Ace Garage, North Circular Road, at about 15 m.p.h.. and close to the nearside kerb, in the direction of Harrow Road.

When 100-150 yards from the Ace Garage he was overtaken by a light-coloured car, the

And, increasingly, the Ace Cafe was mentioned in the reports. This is Ernie with his Ariel Arrow.

speed of which attracted his attention. He had been driving for eight or nine years and estimated the other car's speed at 80 m.p.h..

It was travelling towards its offside kerb and he was not obstructing it as far as he could judge. When it was some distance ahead of him he saw what appeared to be a cloud of smoke or dust come from the offside as if one of the wheels had touched the offside kerb of the central section of the dual carriageway, in the vicinity of the Ace Garage.

The car went out of control and crashed

into a concrete post on the centre section. When it came into collision with the post it appeared to leap into the air and then went into the opposite carriageway, facing at right angles to the road.

He saw a number of people come from the garage and cafe to give assistance, and in those circumstances continued. He did not remember seeing any vehicle between his van and the car at the time it crashed into the kerb of the centre section.

Willesden Chronicle, July 4, 1958

Brian John Howard, aged 21, lorry driver, of Cobbold Road, Harlesden, N.W., who drove along the North Circular Road at midnight at 70 miles an hour, was sentenced to 18 months' imprisonment and disqualified from driving until July 1, 1964, at the Central Criminal Court yesterday. He had pleaded Guilty to causing the death of his friend and passenger, Ralph George Lang, aged 21, of Bryan House, Bryan Avenue, Harlesden, by dangerous driving.

Passing sentence the Lord Chief Justice (Lord Goddard) said: 'The roads of this country, as everyone knows, are strewn with wounded, dead, and dying, and if people drive in the way you were driving no wonder. Parliament has recently passed an Act providing that those who cause death by dangerous driving are liable to be sent to prison for five years. I am not going to send you to prison for five years, but unless the courts pass sharp sentences in these cases so that people who drive in the way that you were driving that night knows what will happen to them if they cause these dreadful disasters of death, this sort of thing will go on.

'You were driving at something like 70 miles an hour on the North Circular Road and it is only by the mercy of Providence that you did not kill other people with your car getting out of control in this way simply because you were driving at this mad dog speed.'

Johnny and Jimmy have a burn-up. After leaving the Ace on the southbound lane, the leading 'Tiger' on his 650cc Ton-ten approaches the Grand Union Canal.

Left: **Exiting on the far side of the aqueduct, the Norton just overtaking the car is hotly pursued by a pair of Vincent 1000s with Rob and Patsy on the right-hand bike.** *Right:* **The original north-bound lane of the North Circular is now used as a local two-way feeder on this side of the road, hence the comparison was taken — not without some risk — standing on the new carriageway.**

Jimmy is now approaching Hangar Lane. In the background the building once occupied by the Fire Auto and Marine insurance company led by Dr Emil Savundra which collapsed in 1967 leaving thousands without insurance cover . . . including Mad Bill!

hitting him or going up the kerb of the centre section in the road so I chose to go up the kerb, intending to stop there. I remember striking the kerb but I cannot remember anything after that.' Howard claimed that he was only doing between 35 and 40 miles an hour.

The Times, July 22, 1958

The annual statistical analysis of road accidents in the Metropolitan Police District reveals that in 1957 more than one person in every thousand of the London population was seriously injured as the result of a road accident. There were 669 deaths — a decrease of 2 per cent compared with the previous year. Casualties to motorcyclists rose by 12.8 per cent to 12,428. It is interesting to note that there were 4,347 fewer accidents in 1957 than in 1938 in spite of greatly increased number of vehicles now on the road.

The Police Review, September 26, 1958

The Parliamentary Secretary of the Ministry of Transport, announced that a short cartoon film on protective helmets for motorcyclists had been commissioned to be shown on television.

Press Report, 1958

Mr. R. E. Seaton, for the prosecution, had said at midnight on May 19 Howard was driving a hired car along the North Circular Road, at Stonebridge, and with him he had four passengers. There was a 40 m.p.h. restriction on this section of dual carriageway which was also well lighted. The defendant passed a car which was towing a broken down vehicle. According to witnesses he was travelling at a tremendous speed and after overtaking he mounted the grass verge dividing the two carriageways and crashed into a lamp-post. All five persons in his car were injured and, as so often happened, Howard, the driver, was hurt least seriously of all. One of the passengers, Mr. Lang, died shortly afterwards.

In a statement the defendant told the police: 'As I was approaching the Ace Cafe I took the outside lane to overtake a black saloon car. As I drove alongside I got the impression that he wanted to play games because instead of letting me pass he stayed level with me. I could not make up my mind whether to accelerate or slow down. Before I could do either he pulled out into the offside lane. I had a choice of

The same spot some 40 years later. On the right No. 56 Waverley Gardens.

Bob Cannall on the Ace forecourt with young Roy in the background.

A chase through Willesden streets of a young Harlesden motorcyclist, during which it was stated a speed of 80 m.p.h. was recorded on the speedometer of a police motorcycle, was described to Willesden magistrates on Monday.

Before the court on summonses for dangerous driving at North Circular Road, Coronation Road and Park Royal Road, Willesden, was Peter William John Windsor, an RAF storeman, of Convent Cottages, Crownhill Road, Harlesden.

Police Constable William Coles said that on June 1 at 4.45 p.m. he saw Windsor riding a motorcycle at Neasden and followed him. Windsor's speed from the Iron Bridge, Neasden, to Harrow Road varied from 65 to 75 m.p.h. Approaching the traffic lights, Windsor slowed down to about 50 m.p.h. and then accelerated away. From Stonebridge railway bridge his speed varied from 70 to 80 m.p.h. and at Hangar Lane, Windsor cut dangerously between stationary cars before turning into Twyford Abbey Road.

'He saw me and accelerated away towards Coronation Road and in Coronation Road his speed was 60 to 75 m.p.h.,' continued the officer. He said that he eventually managed to overtake and stop Windsor near Horn Lane, Acton. The overall distance of the chase was five and one tenth-mile and at the time North Circular Road was very busy and Windsor was swerving in and out of traffic.

'From Hangar Lane on I gathered he was trying to get away from me,' he said.

Windsor, who pleaded guilty, was said to have two motoring convictions. He was fined a total of £25 and ordered to pay £2.12s. 6d. costs. He was disqualified from driving for two years.

Three other motorcyclists were also disqualified from driving by Willesden magistrates on Monday. They were said to have been followed by the police along North Circular Road, Willesden, at a speed varying from 50 to 65 m.p.h.

The first, David Norman Biggs, aged 21, of Christchurch Hill, Hampstead, was fined £15 for driving at a dangerous speed, £3 for exceeding 40 m.p.h. on North Circular Road, and £10 for driving a motorcycle whilst uninsured. He was disqualified from driving for two years.

Similar fines were imposed on Bernard Donovan, aged 18, of Lyndhurst Road, Hampstead, who appeared on summonses for aiding and abetting Biggs and using a motorcycle without insurance. He was also disqualified from driving for two years.

The third youth, Patrick Peter Connors, aged 19, of Compayne Gardens, West Hampstead was fined £15 for driving at a dangerous speed and £3 for exceeding 40 m.p.h. on the North Circular Road. He was disqualified from driving for one year. The three, in addition were each ordered to pay £1 4s. 6d. costs.

The court was told that Biggs was riding one machine with Donovan as pillion passenger and Connors was riding another. Their speed between Normanamead and Durand Way varied from 50 to 65 m.p.h.

'There were a number of children playing on the grass verge and it would have been impossible for either of them to have pulled up in an emergency if the children had run into the road,' said PC Norman Fielding.

Biggs and Connors pleaded not guilty to the summonses for driving at a dangerous speed and said they had control of the machine. 'The road surface was good and I did not see any danger in exceeding the speed limit,' said Connors.

Willesden Chronicle, November 7, 1958

As the firms in the motorcycle industry prepare themselves for a vigorous sales effort at the Cycle and Motor Cycle Show which opens at Earls Court on Saturday, it is timely to consider the fundamental changes that have come over the industry since the war, and what further changes may be forced upon it in the future.

The principal change, of course, has been the advent of the scooter, which was seen here in significant numbers for the first time in 1953, after several years of growing popularity on the Continent.

Another, but less important, change has been caused by the moped. It is fair to say that the British motorcycle firms despised the scooter at first and have largely continued to do so. They could not believe that young men in particular, could possibly be attracted by such low-powered machines, and to some extent they were right — many young men today still favour the 'proper' motorcycle, with its much higher road performance.

What the manufacturers failed to see, however, was that the scooter would attract many men simply as an inexpensive means of transport, and that it would appeal to an entirely new group of owners — women — for whom a conventional motorcycle would be unthinkable.

A favourable development they could not be expected to foresee in 1953 was that a large part of the demand for motorcycles, especially the powerful models of 500 c.c. and over, would henceforth come from young men in the United States, who have also taken so strongly to the British sports car. The motorcycles exported to the United States are used principally for speed competitions, in which they are highly successful.

Just how fortunate the British motorcycle industry has been in this respect can be seen by comparing the number of machines of over 250 c.c. registered in Britain last year (30,063) with the number of machines, mostly 500s, exported to the United States (12,303).

In 1953 the total British production of 154,100 motorcycles included some 7,500 scooters, and a further 1,400 scooters were imported. Last year the total production of 175,000 motorcycles included 31,000 scooters, and a further 69,000 were imported.

There is little doubt that the fine spring and early summer of 1957 encouraged many people to buy scooters just as the rainy summer this year has been a deterrent.

A nice Triumph — note the early chain case and '57 front wheel. On the left with his head down, Bob readies his own machine.

It should perhaps be emphasized that in Britain the moped, although the product of the cycle industry, is treated as a motorcycle as regards the need for a driving licence, tax and insurance. Raleigh consider the production of a moped as a logical step from the manufacture of bicycles, but claim that cycle manufacture will be in no way affected, they anticipate that moped sales will supplement those of bicycles rather than compete with them. Meanwhile, the manufacturers of 'real' motorcycles, apart from entering the scooter market, have done much to bring the comfort of their machines, particularly as regards weather protection, up to scooter standard.

Looking to the future, in spite of the unprecedented rate of road construction and improvement, traffic congestion in cities and towns is certain to get worse and public transport fares continue at a high level — two conditions that should ensure a steadily expanding market for the motorcycle industry as a whole.

The Times, November 11, 1958

A Kensal Green motorcyclist involved in a crash on the North Circular Road, Neasden, was sent for trial at the Old Bailey when he appeared at Willesden on Monday.

Roger George Williams, aged 18, Post Office clerk of Rainham Road, was charged with causing the death of his pillion passenger, David Foster, aged 18, of Hawthorne Grove Kingsbury, by dangerous driving. Mr. Foster died in Central Middlesex Hospital of injuries nine days after the accident.

Witnesses stated that the motorcycle was being driven at high speed near the Book Centre, at about 10.40 p.m. on September 24, and after a mishap went into the opposite carriageway and crashed into an oncoming car.

Alan James Bennett, of Sutton Road, Muswell Hill, said that a number of motorcycles passed his car as he was travelling north beyond the Stonebridge crossing lights. At one time, three of them were abreast ahead of him and talking to one another. He overtook them at about 40 miles an hour near a railway bridge, and then about six motorcycles passed him again at a much higher speed in single file.

Mr. Bennett said there was a gap between the last motorcycle and his car and then another machine with two men on it passed him at about 60 miles an hour. This machine tried to negotiate the beginning of the left hand curve at the foot of the bridge, failed to do so and mounted the kerb at an intersection. There was a shower of sparks as the machine apparently hit a post at the intersection and then it shot into the oncoming lane.

John Joseph O'Connor, of Rosebank Avenue, Sudbury Hill, said he was driving towards Stonebridge at 35 to 40 miles an hour when he saw a lot of motorcycles going up the other carriageway. One came across the intersection at 'terrific speed'. He braked violently and stopped and the motorcycle struck the wing and driver's door of his car.

Peter John Wakelin, of Bridge Road, Neasden, said he was walking along on the Book Centre side when two or three motorcycles passed at high speed. Then another motorcycle, which seemed as if it was trying to catch the others, approached at about 70 to 80 miles an hour. It was going into the bend past Ascot's when it struck the edge of the intersection, crossed the intersection and hit the other side, then went into the other carriageway.

Willesden Chronicle, November 21, 1958

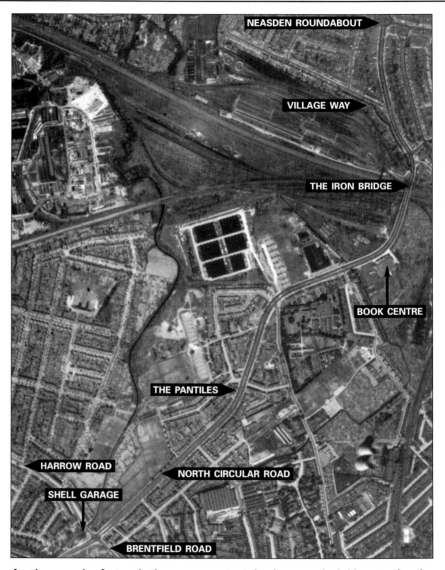

Another recurring feature in the press reports at the time was the bridge crossing the Metropolitan and Bakerloo lines at Neasden dubbed 'the Iron Bridge'. When approaching from the Ace, a fast right-hander led to a 40-degree bend to the left to cross the bridge which exited around another 40-degree left-hander to the long curve up to the Neasden roundabout. David Foster was fatally injured there on September 24, 1958.

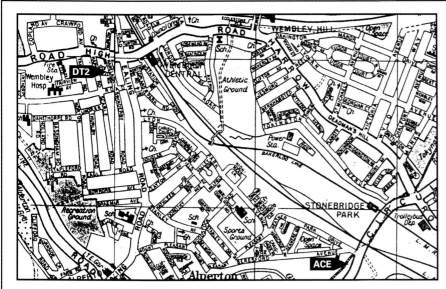

obvious that the riders were racing. The police car gave chase and speeds of 70-75 m.p.h. were recorded. At the junction of North Circular Road and Harrow Road the traffic lights were red and the three motorcyclists braked hard and stopped.

The police car drew alongside them, continued Mr. Rogers, and the three riders, two of whom were Whitcombe and Allnutt, were told to pull round the corner as the officers wishes to speak to them. Allnutt did so, but Whitcombe and the other man rode off. Whitcombe was followed to the Ace Cafe and the police car came up as he was dismounting. Whitcombe's machine had attained 70 m.p.h. between Harrow Road and the cafe.

Mr. Rogers said Whitcombe refused his name and address and was taken to Wembley Police Station. There he did give his particulars and admitted ownership of the machine.

Allnutt was seen later and he said, 'I admit I was riding very fast and may have been doing 70 m.p.h.'

Willesden Chronicle, March 20, 1959

In those days, the Metropolitan Police were divided up into four districts each with their own district traffic patrols and transport garage. District Transport 2 — DT2 — covered north and north-west London like the slice of a cake with the point at Marble Arch, opening out to Uxbridge, Harrow and Ruislip.

The section of the North Circular bordering the Ace was covered from DT2 which lay in Ranelagh Road — a turning off Wembley High Road. The old police station on the corner still stands although the garage behind has since been demolished and redeveloped with flats.

A race between three motorcycles at North Circular Road, Willesden, in which speeds of 70 to 75 m.p.h. were recorded by a following police car, was described by Mr. John Rogers, prosecuting, at Willesden Court on Monday.

Two of the motorcyclists, Michael Anthony Whitcombe, of Hillcrest, Hatfield, Herts., and Donald Alfred Allnutt, of St. John's Road, Isleworth, were summoned for driving at a dangerous speed and over the permitted 40 m.p.h. Whitcombe was further summoned for failing to stop when requested by a uniformed policeman, refusing to give his name and address and driving a motorcycle without proper illumination of an index plate.

Mr. Rogers told the magistrates that on October 25 last year a patrol car drew up at the traffic lights at Brentfield Road and North Circular Road. On the stop line in front of them they saw three motorcyclists abreast of each other and decided to take their numbers.

When the lights changed, the three machines raced off down the road and it was

73

Officers had to be Class 1 or 2 drivers to work on the Traffic Division, and DT2 was equipped with Wolseleys and and Triumph Speed Twin 500s. (Class 3 drivers could work on wireless cars, Class 4 vans and cars without radio, and Class 5 — the lowest — the station hack!) Traffic police worked a month about between cars and motorcycles. This beautiful shot of a DT2 Wolseley 6/90 was provided by ex-PC Tony Purbrick who was stationed there from 1957 to 1966.

From time to time the complaint of extravagance is made when a Chief Constable proposes that his Force should be equipped with patrol cars of high quality. The members of Police Authorities who make these complaints are probably drivers of limited experience who cannot understand why what is good enough for them is not good enough for the Police. Factors which are overlooked are the very big mileages undertaken by Police cars, and the occasions when road-holding, brakes, acceleration and speed must all be of a high standard if a motor patrol is to have a fair chance of succeeding in its task.

Mr. H. R. Pratt, the Chief Constable of Bedfordshire, had to stress these points when he recently put forward a proposal to the Standing joint Committee that four Ford Zephyr patrol cars should be replaced with

four Jaguar 2.4 saloons. Some members of the Committee thought the cheaper car was quite good enough, and that the expenditure of an additional £500 on each Jaguar could not be justified.

Mr. Pratt's reply to this was that the Police needed a car with outstandingly good road-holding qualities which was also capable of the speeds needed to catch some offenders. He also said it was estimated that the Jaguars would last almost twice as long as the Fords, and this would help to meet the additional cost.

In spite of this explanation some members of the Committee remained unconvinced. One of them went so far as to question the need for any cars at all. Why could not motorcycles be used instead? he asked.

Mr. Pratt came down hard on this. motorcycles were most unpleasant to drive in bad weather, he said, and in his opinion were highly dangerous things. He did not like to see Police officers riding them. When equipped with wireless they carried it in a bulky container at the rear, and this made the machines unwieldy and unstable.

Mr. Pratt's arguments won the day. He is to have his Jaguars and we are sure his Force will be the better for them. Quality counts when a car has to do what may be required of it on Police duty.

The Police Review, April 17, 1959

We discovered that the picture was taken in Floriston Close, Stanmore, a cul-de-sac off Weston Drive where the crew had been dealing with an accident enquiry.

Sergeant Len Farmer, the instructor on the Thunderbird, with Tony (front left), Ronnie Askham and Brian Skelton.

The driver of a laundry van that was involved in a fatal accident with a motorcyclist at the junction of Crest Road and Brook Road, Neasden, on March 6 did not appear at the Kilburn inquest on Tuesday.

The inquest was on 19-year-old Geoffrey Paul, a refrigerator technician, of 90 Church Road, Willesden. The jury returned a verdict of accidental death.

Mr. Hector Coffey, brother-in-law of Mr. Paul, said Geoffrey Paul had been riding the motorcycle for about three months and held a provisional licence.

Mr. Vivian Paul, a cousin of the dead man, said he was a pillion passenger on the motorcycle when the collision happened. They were going home from work. As they approached the junction of Crest Road from Brook Road, their speed was about 30 m.p.h. Nearing the junction, Geoffrey changed gear and tried to slow down to make the right turn into Crest Road. He might not have slowed down enough — if they had taken the turn their speed would have been in the region of 25 m.p.h. He could remember nothing about the accident.

Mr. Albert Neal, an employee of Westerns Laundries Ltd, Holloway Road, said he was in the van at the time. They were travelling at about 25 m.p.h. along Crest Road towards Edgware Road. When they got about half way across the junction with Brook Road, there was a bang against the side of the van. They pulled up and saw the motorcyclist lying on the road.

Two women, who were waiting at a bus stop at the time, also gave evidence and said the motorcycle 'appeared to come from nowhere all of a sudden' as the van was half way across the mouth of the junction.

Willesden Chronicle, April 3, 1959

A big increase in traffic on main roads in July, compared with the same month last year, was accompanied by a further sharp rise in road casualties, the Ministry of Transport and Civil Aviation announced yesterday.

The most serious increase was once more in casualties to riders of motorcycles, including motor-scooters, and their passengers. These were 10,513, an increase of 2,450, or over 30 per cent. More than 200 of these riders and passengers lost their lives. The total of 531 casualties to moped riders is nearly double the July 1958, figure and includes 14 deaths as compared with one a year ago.

Casualties to drivers of other motor vehicles and their passengers numbered 10,994, an increase of 1,036. There were 155 deaths.

Sixty-four pedal cyclists were killed; an increase of two.

The Times, September 9, 1959

Sir, — Your Motoring Correspondent in his recent article did well to draw the attention of manufacturers of motorbicycles and scooters to the menace of the everlasting increase in the power and speed of these machines.

The monthly statistics of road accidents confirm the experience of motorists. Week by week the number of motorbicycles and scooters increases. What is worse, new models are advertised as possessing greater power and, consequently, higher speeds. One gains the impression that the majority of these machines are purchased by boys in their teens. Full employment at high wages, together with hire-purchase terms, has resulted in boys who a few years ago were content with pedal bicycles charging around the country at very high speeds. In many cases they have not even taken the test, and many do not trouble to do so.

An investigation into the average age of motorcyclists would provide interesting statistics, especially if it could be related to the accident figures. I recently met, in hospital, a boy of 19 who was recovering from his third serious smash. He boasted to me of his exploits when out with his friends when speeds of 85 miles per hour are common and he confessed that he had touched 109 miles per hour on one occasion. He assured me, however, that he was very careful when he had his girlfriend on the pillion, when he never exceeded 65 miles per hour!

Yours faithfully,

ANTHONY THOMAS
Queen's Head Cottages, Wittersham, Kent

The Times, September 9, 1959

Sir, — The menace on two wheels, described by Mr. Thomas in his letter today, will continue to grow if only because fast motorcycling is so downright exciting. I once heard it compared with piloting a Spitfire at low altitudes.

I imagine there are few young men who can resist the experience when offered to them. But very few have received a tithe of the instruction given to a Spitfire pilot and equally few possess comparable skill. And here I believe the law could help by limiting the use of high-powered motorcycles to people with a modicum of experience and skill. After all, no complete novice can tie 'L' plates on to a Spitfire and take off. But there is nothing to prevent a youth of 16 of 17 putting 'L' plates on a machine capable of 100 miles per hour and setting off for the other side of England. He need have had no instruction at all. He only needs to say that he can read a car number plate at 25 yards and that he has studied the Highway Code.

Surely this is a disgraceful state of affairs. It ought not to be beyond the power of Parliament to pass some simple legislation restricting the novice to low-powered machines (say under 150 c.c.) and to insist on minimum age and experience before he goes on to anything bigger. No one wants more complicated laws, but I believe that in the

laws granting licences to motorcyclists and potential motorcyclists there is room for considerable elaboration in the cause of road safety. Better to sort it out this way than to leave it to the magistrate's court, the hospital, or the mortuary.

Yours faithfullly,
PETER IENT
The Parsonage, Eastfield, Scarborough

The Times, September 11, 1959

Sir, — Further to the letter today from the Rev. Peter Ient on 'the menace' of boys of 16 and 17 on high-powered motorcycles (and it is surely a tragedy as well as a menace), during the passage of the Road Traffic Act through the House of Lords in 1956, I moved an amendment to clause 10, to provide that 'any licence . . . granted to a person under the age of 18 years shall exclude a licence to drive a motorcycle having an engine power in excess of 250 c.c. capacity'; and I explained that if I had thought there was any prospect of the Government's accepting it I would

have made my amendment a good deal more drastic, but that at least it would prevent mere boys from riding machines of 500 or 1,000 c.c.

The Government spokesman professed the general sympathy with the aims of the

amendment with which those who campaign for road safety are all too familiar, and went on to object (1) that probably 'the chief dangers come to and from those a little older' than 16 to 18, (2) that in view of possible engineering progress it would be unwise to impose a 250 c.c. or any other, limit, and (3), the familiar trump card, that a departmental committee on road safety was sitting, and when it had reported the Minister would decide what to do — and his action, which might be taken by way of regulations, 'may well be a great deal more drastic' than the amendment.

That was in July 1956. The committee reported in July 1957. Since then no action, drastic or otherwise, has been taken, but statistics, I understand, are being, or have been, collected. Meanwhile the toll of life and limb continues.

I am, Sir, yours &c.   ELTON
Adderbury, near Banbury, Oxfordshire

The Times, September 14, 1959

A verdict of Accidental Death was returned by the jury at an inquest at Hendon on Thursday on 23-year-old Mr. Brian Webster, of 72, Paxford Road, North Wembley, who died after injuries received in an accident at Kenton Road, Kenton, on September 23.

It was said that Mr. Webster's motorcycle was in collision with a motorcycle combination, slewed across the road and crashed into the front of a van.

Harrow Observer, October 29, 1959

A fight in the Ace Cafe, Stonebridge Park, during which a police sergeant was punched and kicked and pushed into a window, breaking it, was described to Harrow magistrates on Friday.

Two Harlesden youths, Peter John Lee, aged 17, driver, of Shakespeare Avenue, and Peter James Reynard, aged 20, driver, of Wyborne Way, were charged with assaulting Police Sergeant Richard Britt.

Sergeant Britt said he went with PC Godfrey Tearle to the Ace Cafe at 11 p.m. on November 5 and saw a crowd of youths, among whom were the two accused, throwing food about.

Sergeant. Britt spoke to the manager and then went up to the table where the youths were sitting. As he did so, one of them threw some sauce from a bottle over Lee.

'I said to Reynard he had been asked to leave and he had better go now,' said the sergeant, and he said, '— off, or try and put me out.' As he said this he kicked me in the shins, and when I closed with him he punched me in the side.

'As we struggled, a number of youths gathered round and aimed punches at me. One of them tried to hit me over the head with a sauce bottle. Lee punching me on the right side of the neck.

'After a time, Reynard said, 'All right I will swallow it,' and stopped fighting. I went to take him from the cafe and he pushed me into a window, breaking it. I closed with him again, and we fought our way outside the cafe.'

Sergeant Britt said that outside the cafe Lee grabbed hold of his left arm and tried to jerk him to the ground. Reynard broke away and ran off, pursued by PC Tearle.

The sergeant took Lee to a police car which had arrived and then went after Reynard. PC Tearle had arrested him, and he was also put in the car.

'They continued to struggle and fight violently in the car and at the police station,' said the sergeant.

Reynard told the court he was very sorry. 'I apologise to the police and cafe manager,' he said. 'It was a very silly thing to do, but I wasn't in my right mind. I had been drinking.'

Lee was said to have two findings of guilt, one of them for insulting behaviour, recorded against him and Reynard two previous convictions, one for obstructing the footway and one for insulting words and behaviour.

Willesden Chronicle, November 13, 1959

Julie can be recognised at the table while Chrissy is about to feed the jukebox.

'Let's go and take a motorbike for a laugh', one of a gang of youths said to his friends late one night in Stonebridge.

This suggestion landed two Stonebridge boys, aged 15 and 16, in Willesden Juvenile Court accused of taking and driving away a two-stroke motorcycle and having no insurance policies.

A police officer said he was driving along on a motorcycle at 11.20 p.m. on November 27 when he saw one of the youths astride the vehicle and the other pushing it. He drew up and asked them if they had a licence.

'They looked very frightened and said "no",' he explained. Then the boys dropped the machine and ran off. The officer gave chase and caught one of them, who said:

'I didn't nick it.' The second youth had been arrested at his home later.

The elder boy told the bench: 'We were in a cafe in Stonebridge and after it closed I came out with all my mates — there was a great gang of them.' Then one made the suggestion.

They found a motorcycle and four of them climbed on it, he said, and then he went on: 'It wouldn't start. They threw it in the middle of the road and walked off. I thought it might cause an accident and so I said to my friend, "Let's take it back." I was sitting on it and he was pushing when the policeman suddenly jumped on me.

Willesden Chronicle, December 11, 1959

Road, near North Circular Road. Whenever his car came abreast, giving signals to stop, the other car drew out, forcing the police car to fall behind.

A motorist had to take violent evasive action when the pursued car crossed a junction against the lights, and another police car had to take avoiding action when the car drove straight towards it.

PC William Foster said he dragged the boy from the driving seat when the car was forced to stop. He struggled until he was put into a police car.

When the schoolboy gave evidence, he could not read the oath card. He said that he was asked in the Ace Cafe to get a car. Not wanting to be 'chicken,' he took one. They took turns at the wheel and then returned to the cafe. They then drove to the Busy Bee Cafe at Watford.

The boy said he realised that a police car was behind them on the journey to London, but he did not know it was signalling him to stop. When he wanted to stop, Keithlow pushed the throttle and made him go on.

When the chase was on, he and the others told the driver to stop, but he said it was better to go on than to be caught. He did not know the car was not the schoolboy's, and he thought he was older than 15.

Willesden Chronicle, December 18, 1959

Forty years separate these two pictures of the famous front wall at the Ace.

A three-mile chase through Finchley of a car driven by a schoolboy aged 15 was described to Willesden magistrates by six police officers on Monday.

Throughout the chase at 5.30 on Sunday morning, two police cars rang bells and flashed lights, and one came abreast seven times; but the pursued car refused to stop until a police car drove across the bonnet.

Four youths appeared in court. The schoolboy pleaded guilty to driving while disqualified by age and while uninsured, and not guilty to taking and driving away a car without the owner's consent.

Mr. William Hannington, of Clematis Street, Shepherds Bush, said he left his £500 car outside the Ace Cafe, North Circular Road, at 2.15 a.m. When he came out after a cup of tea it had gone.

PC Kenneth Swinden said the chase started in Ballards Lane, and ended in Finchley

The hunters . . . and the hunted. This specially-equipped TAG Humber [Traffic Accident Goup car] was pictured at the Target pub roundabout at Northolt. L-R: John Hooper, Stan Bayley, Ray Schilder and Tony Purbrick.

The problem of accidents involving motorcyclists is a serious one. Every month large numbers of motorcyclists are killed or injured, and the figures reach alarming proportions. As these accidents have to be dealt with by policemen we may be justly disturbed by the amount of work these accidents cause us, but our concern should be much deeper than this.

The motorcycle by its very construction is vulnerable, and so of course is the rider therefore when involved in an accident, regardless of who is to blame, the motorcyclist usually comes off badly. There can be no doubt that the modern motorcycle is a popular means of transport, whether it be the little two-stroke on which Dad goes to the office each day, the scooter which Susie diligently polishes but hasn't a clue how it works, or the powerful 'road burner' that is Bill's pride and joy. This popularity is understandable and justified.

It is easy to say 'But what can we do about it?' as the carnage goes on. The average motorcyclist is a nice chap, too nice to be killed or injured just because his mode of transport is a motorcycle. We can put motorcyclists in the book for everything we can think of, but I doubt if that is any good. In fact, I suspect it does very little to reduce the casualties.

The Chief Constable of Devon has said that we must tie them to our apron strings. Well, if only for their own good that might be an idea. But how? They need some sort of help or protection, but it must be done on a worth-while scale.

The ACU/RAC motorcycle training schemes are excellent in both concept and practice. They rely on the voluntary instruction of members of local motorcycle clubs, and many manufacturers have assisted with generous gifts of motorcycles for the pupils' use.

Now, this business of instruction by members of local motorcycle clubs is surely a pointer in the right direction, for a motorcyclist is most likely to listen to another motorcyclist — someone who talks his language, understands his problems and, above all else, is one of his clan.

The man on the beat or on motor patrol may stop an erring motorcyclist and point out to him the error of his ways, but does he pay any heed? I venture to suggest that the average motorcyclist would pay far more attention to a police motorcyclist. I do not mean simply a policeman on a motorcycle. What I mean is a policeman who is a first-class motorcyclist and a motorcycling enthusiast: a chap who knows his motorcycles and also the fellows (and ladies) who ride them.

All too often we hear the excuse, 'Honestly, I can't keep her under thirty in top, officer.' But if the erring motorcyclist realised he was talking to someone who knew as much as he did about motorcycles — perhaps more — then he would think twice before trotting out any feeble excuses, and instead he would listen and learn from what he was told, appreciating the fact that the officer was no fool when it came to the subject of owning and riding motorcycles.

A friendly talk or natter with such a police motorcyclist could do nothing but good, for soon it would get around that the officer was 'one of them.' He would be listened to with far more interest than an officer who has ridden nothing more potent than a pedal-cycle, yet presumes he is a fit person to tell someone how to ride a powerful motorcycle.

Let our police motorcycling be of the highest possible standard; let it set an example to other motorcyclists. Show them that a motorcycle properly ridden can be a safe, efficient means of transport; show them that good motorcycling can be *fast* motorcycling but is essentially *safe* motorcycling.

The sight of a police motorcyclist riding in an impeccable manner would not only act as a deterrent to any would-be transgressor, but would be a demonstration of how motorcycling should be done. I am quite sure that motorcyclists would take notice of such good motorcycling and that there would be a favourable reaction. It is not good enough to ride around 'any old how' on a police motorcycle just looking for offences. Much more can be done with the machine and your time.

The laws of this country do not help, for it is clearly idiotic that a person can pass a driving test on a 50 c.c. moped and immediately roar off on a highly powered machine. We can do little about that, but I am sure that police motorcyclists, who are themselves motorcycling enthusiasts, can do a great deal to reduce the frightening toll which is exacted from among fellow motorcyclists.

Good advice, given in a proper manner by someone well qualified, and the continued demonstration of good motorcycling, would be a step in the right direction. Recently the Editor of one of the leading motorcycling magazines told me that in his experience road safety had to be fed quietly to motorcyclists. Other methods did not work. Well, it could be 'fed quietly' by police motorcyclists who could prove that motorcycles are not just noisy and dangerous machines ridden by maniacs.

The Police Review, January 15, 1960

The text of Vice-Admiral Hughes Hallett's Bill to prevent inexperienced riders from using powerful motorcycles was published yesterday. It is a private member's Bill which is due to come up for second reading on March 4.

It would limit the granting of a licence to drive a motorcycle of over 250 c.c. to people who are over 17 and who have had one year's experience in riding less powerful motorcycles. The Minister of Transport would be given power to lower the age (now 16) at which young people can ride mopeds to 15. The Bill is called the Road Traffic (Driving of Motor Cycles and Mopeds) Bill.

The Times, January 30, 1960

The second reading of the Road Traffic (Driving of Motor Cycles and Mopeds) Bill was resumed. The Bill limits the use of machines over 250 c.c. to experienced riders.

Mr. Hay, Parliamentary Secretary, Ministry of Transport said they had now received the results of the survey into the causes of motorcycle accidents. They did show, to some extent, support for the conception used as a bases for this Bill — that experience of driving these machines was likely to be more significant than age.

The Times, May 14, 1960

So far so good, but still not far enough, would be a just description of the Road Traffic (Driving of Motor Cycles and Mopeds) Bill, which completed its second reading on Friday. This measure, the work of Vice-Admiral Hughes Hallett, would restrict the driving of a heavy motorcycle to a person who has held a full and unendorsed licence to drive a light one for at least a year. The need for action was plain. Last year the number of mopeds involved in accidents rose by nearly 78 per cent; with motor-scooters and motorcycles the increase was of the order of 20 per cent. In signifying the decision of the Government not to oppose the Bill, Mr. Hay properly called these figures staggering and disastrous. He agreed that something had to be done to put these things right.

Will this Bill 'put things right?' Though it is largely in line with the recommendations of the Committee on Road Safety in 1957, that seems doubtful.

There is surely a good case for raising the minimum age for driving any sort of motorcycle. The Minister already has the power to do so under Section 10 of the Road Traffic Act of 1956, but he has not chosen to take advantage of it. The present Bill, in so far as it affects this authority at all, does so only to enable him to reduce the minimum to 15 in the case of mopeds. The implicit principle of graduating from less to more powerful machines is excellent, but is 15 or even 16 a safe starting point?

The Times, May 16, 1960

The quarry prepare to enjoy themselves in a burn-up on the North Circular.

Servicing the bikes in the pits before the next race. Unfortunately the lad with his head down on the left cannot be identified but next to him behind the Tiger Cub is Bob Cannall; Derek Ingham; Alan 'Kipper' Fisher working on the Triumph; unidentified; Jeff Lavis and, on the extreme right, Noddy's best mate Mad Bill.

Learner-driver Eric Arthur Sampson, aged 19, electrician's mate, drove a motorcycle at 62-70 m.p.h. along busy Harrow Road, Willesden, only 10 days after taking out a provisional licence.

Describing him as a 'menace' on the road, the chairman of Willesden Bench (Mr. I. J. Sparke) on Monday fined him £25 for driving at a dangerous speed on July 25. Sampson, of Herries Street, Queen's Park, was disqualified for three years.

PC John Barber said that while on motor-cycle duty he chased Sampson's motorcycle in Harrow Road from Conduit Way to Craven Park. During the chase when Sampson touched 70 m.p.h. he passed nine road junctions and several pedestrian crossings. There were all kinds of driving hazards, such as parked vehicles, pedestrians, children and animals.

Willesden Chronicle, August 12, 1960

Three young men died in road accidents in the Willesden area this week — one on a motorcycle on the North Circular Road, on Sunday; another motorcyclist, a young police-man, was fatally injured at Manor Park Road, Harlesden, on Saturday; and the rider of a motor scooter died in hospital on Wednesday following a crash at Old Oak Common Lane, Willesden, on Tuesday afternoon.

Willesden Chronicle, September 9, 1960

Two motorcyclists and their pillion passen-gers were injured on the North Circular Road when they were involved in a collision with a car. The car driver was Mr. John Chandler, of Cairnfield Avenue, Neasden, and the collision occurred near Brendon Avenue. Those injured were: Mr. Michael Pasqua, 20, and Miss Carol Davies, 16, of Kingsbury, and Colin Mann, 21, and Gerald Smart, 19, of Middlesex.

Willesden Citizen, December 2, 1960

Above: **Bob 'Tiny' Griffiths, left foreground on bike, with friends at the Scrubs Fair in March 1959. The following year he was killed at The Pantiles (see also page 49).**
Below: **Tiny was taken to Carpenders Park Lawn Cemetery in Oxhey Lane, Watford, and laid to rest in Grave 177 of Section C.**

Two died as the result of another crash on the North Circular Road, Willesden, on Thursday last week. They were Mr. Robert Victor Griffiths, 20-year-old motorcyclist of 97 Harrow Road, Wembley, and his pillion passenger, Mr. David William Lambert, aged 23, 0f 4 Marley Close, Greenford.

Mr. Griffiths is believed to have swerved to avoid another vehicle near Ascot Park and his machine hit the kerb. He was thrown onto the verge and Mr. Lambert was found lying in the road.

Willesden Chronicle, November 18, 1960

Two young men, one from Tokyngton and the other from Greenford, died after a motorcycle crash on the North Circular Road, Neasden. A verdict of accidental death was returned by a jury at an Ealing inquest last week, when another motorcyclist estimated their speed at about 75 m.p.h.

The inquest was into the death of Robert Victor Griffiths, a driver of 97 Harrow Road, Tokyngton, and David Lambert, a factory hand of 4 Marley Close, Greenford. The accident was on November 10.

Mr. Albert Griffiths said that his son, who was riding the machine, had been driving motorcycles for at least three years and had bought this machine secondhand about six months ago. He said his son knew the North Circular Road very well.

Mr. Bryan Newman of 236 North Circular Road, Neasden, said: 'At about 8.30 p.m. I was standing on the corner of St Raphael's Way. I saw sparks coming from a motorcycle as it came round a bend in the road, and as it approached the traffic lights, which were green, I saw a van moving very slowly out into the carriageway from a gap in the centre island. As soon as the motorcyclist saw the van he pulled over to his left-hand kerb and went between the van and the kerb.'

Mr. Newman said after passing the van the motorcyclist tried to straighten up but crashed.

Mr. David Silence of Oxgate Gardens, Cricklewood, said he was riding his motorcycle at about 40 m.p.h. along the North Circular Road. 'As I approached The Pantiles another machine overtook me at about 75 to 80 m.p.h., swerved in front of a van coming out of an opening in the dual carriageway, and crashed against the kerb or a lamp-post on the left-hand side of the road.'

The van driver, Mr. John Baldwin of Colindale Avenue, Colindale, said he turned his van into an opening of the centre island, intending to go back the way he had come.

'Before moving out into the other carriageway,' he said, 'I looked through the van window and made sure the road was clear. I had a view of about 100 yards. After turning, I had almost straightened up on the other carriageway when the motorcycle passed in front of me. It was going very fast and it grazed the left-hand kerb, clung to it for about 30 to 35 yards, then crashed, throwing its riders into the air.'

Wembley Observer, December 15, 1960

Today

THE NEW JOHN BULL

Week ending January 14, 1961
Every Tuesday Fourpence

YOUR JOB—and the CAR CRISIS
SPECIAL
INVESTIGATION
INSIDE

The ton-kids' creed:
**LIVE FAST
LOVE HARD
DIE YOUNG**
See page 11

On January 14, 1961 two very significant events occurred which were to have serious repercussions at the Ace. That Saturday morning the new issue of *Today* magazine featured the boys and girls at the café under the banner headline: 'Live fast, Love hard, Die young'. Featured on the cover was Jenny Burton. 'People were always coming down to the Ace taking pictures and I was chosen as I was the one girl with a motorcycle. When this picture was taken I was only 15. They greased my hair and did make-up. They posed the shot by putting the Journey's End poster over a map and getting the head boy at my school — Pound Lane Secondary Modern in Willesden — to put his arm round me. I had had a crash a couple of weeks earlier in Heather Park Road behind the Ace when I came off my Tiger Cub and hit my head. You can see the mark on the helmet I am holding. The other boy on the left also went to my school.'

There are teddy boys, yoblets, beatniks, students — and those terrifying characters normally seen crouched low over roaring machines chasing the curves of the road: the motorcyclists.

They do not embark on orgies of crime, thrive on promiscuity or indulge in childish university pranks. They simply own motorbikes on which they are able to do a ton — a hundred miles an hour — and go for burn-ups. But sometimes the ton is fatal; sometimes the burn-up ends in death.

Just what is the fascination that motorcycling holds for the modern teen-generation? Is it the love of speed? A death wish? Or simply the need for an exciting hobby in an age of jets and jukeboxes?

Off London's North Circular Road, near Stonebridge Park Station, is a place called the Ace Café. Clustered round the building, like horses tethered at the rails of old-time Western saloons, are the mechanical steeds of these coffee-bar cowboys. Inside the café are about a dozen long tables, with swing-out chairs attached to the legs. There is a jukebox.

On a wall the manager has pinned up a letter. It is from a mother thanking the boys in the café who bought a wreath for her son's funeral. He was killed on his bike just a few yards from the Ace.

To hear these kids as they really are, I went along to the café and met a group of them.

There was Reg, a tough-looking 20-year-old; Jeanette, a pretty girl of 18 who rides pillion on her boyfriend's bike; 16-year-old Mary; and Bob, a nervous boy with sharp features and sideburns.

Half a dozen others chipped into the conversation. One of them, his fair hair cropped in an Adam Faith style, started the ball rolling:

'You want to know our motto? It's Live Fast, Love Hard and Die Young!'

'I don't know about that,' said Reg. 'It's a bug. Once you get the urge for speed, you can't lose it. I bought a 250 c.c. first; I belted it so much it blew up. But I had to keep up with my mates.

'We come in here seven nights a week. I bet none of us could show you a pound note. Motorcycling is expensive. We've got no other hobbies, but we might go to parties now and then. A bike keeps us occupied — in between visits to hospital!!

'Take these tales of chicken runs. I've heard of two fellows racing towards each other on the white line on the crown of a road. They say that some drivers, for a dare, will try to change places with their pillion riders while belting along at speed.

'That's plain stupid. We think too much of our bikes for chicken runs. 'Mind you, we do have burn-ups. The satisfaction of a burn-up is proving your bike and yourself are better than the others. There is skill in it as well, especially through traffic. A smaller bike ridden well can often beat a bigger one.

'All this nonsense that people talk about the ton as though it's something magic! There's nothing to it. Every single person with a decent bike has done the ton.

'There's much more fun in going for a burn-up at 70 miles an hour through winding roads than doing a hundred along a straight stretch.'

'The first time I done it, I was disappointed,' Jeanette said.

There were two other girls round our table. 'Well, birds are part of the scene,' Bob commented. 'I reckon birds are braver than blokes. They put up with riding on the back of a bike. I wouldn't. But a bird makes a bad driver. I've had four accidents, three of them with women.'

'What about that accident I had a few weeks back?' said someone. 'I was burning it up a three-lane carriageway chatting with my mate. Suddenly it changed to two lanes and I shot up a wall. Business!'

Young Mary has just bought a bike of her own. Its maximum speed is 85 m.p.h.: 'I don't know why I prefer bikes to dances and records and that. I suppose I'm just not a girl somehow.'

'I've only worn a suit twice in the past year,' said Bob. 'Once to a wedding and once to a funeral. The rest of the time it's been the uniform — jacket, jeans, crash helmet and calf-length boots.'

'I've got a pair of Third Reich boots from a German officer,' said Reg. 'Look like Farmer Giles!'

'Of course, our parents worry about it,' added Bob. 'I've got a 500 c.c.; I've had 98 miles an hour on the clock in third gear. I earned the money to buy it, but my parents still aren't too keen. 'They lie awake each night until I come home. And usually I don't

The 'Journey's End' poster featuring what appear to be two 1950-era Alvis's and a rider on a Matchless — Matchboxes as they were referred to by the boys — was produced by Roland Davies.

get back till the early morning.'

A boy called George joined us. He's the proud owner of a 650 c.c. machine; he claims he's done 114 m.p.h. on it. 'If you're going to write about us,' he said, 'why don't you come for a burn-up?'

Someone plonked a crash helmet on my head, and strapped it up under my chin. I wrapped a scarf round my throat as I watched George kick the machine into life. Then I climbed on.

With a clout of power the bike shot away from the Ace, over the car park and on to the road. The sudden acceleration nearly threw me off. I decided for safety to clutch George's waist. He drove slowly, well within the speed limit. As we went along the North Circular, he pointed out the places where friends of his had been killed or injured.

Bob and Reg were riding on either side. We went under the arches near the café, crossed the Iron Bridge and up to the traffic lights. At the lights, we changed into the opposite lane for the run back. Bob had a word with George. George turned to me: 'Hang on now, I'm going to pull away a bit sharpish.'

The three bikes were set across the road waiting for the lights to change. Red . . . red amber: the bike leaped away, power almost prising me from the seat. Bob and Reg were just in front; we were hammering along trying to catch them. Not a guided tour of the North Circular death-traps now. This was a burn-up.

We hurtled round bends, George laying the bike fantastically near to the ground. A shower of sparks from a scraping foot-rest blazed our trail. As the ground raced by and we chased after the others, I was gripped by the surge of speed. My feet tingled on the foot-rests; I think I stopped breathing.

The run was short. Just as I was losing all sense of belonging, George changed gear and we drew up at the café. We were surrounded.

'Did you do a ton?'

'Eighty-five, said George unhappily. 'My clutch was slipping.'

Holding grimly on the back of a bike cannot be real motorcycling. But I think in that short burn-up I had glimpsed something that inspires these young riders to their fanatical love of motorcycling. This is something which cannot be put into words, only felt on the seat of a bike roaring along a highway.

I went inside for a cup of tea. Speedy, as he is known, is one of the favourite characters of the café. Although he is small, he assured me he was seventeen.

'I started with a scooter,' he said, 'then I began to get the urge. I bought a bike, but that only did 80. I tried a 500 c.c. and now I've got a 600. I just want to go faster all the time, not only on the straight but hammering round bends as well with everything scraping.

'There's a boy comes in here that we call Dave-the-Grave. Why? Because it's a dead cert he's going there. On his shoulders — on his jacket, like — he's got written "To the Death". He means it.

'The others don't reckon I'll last long. But it's a bit of hard luck, isn't it? It doesn't worry me. I mean death's quick, you don't know anything. You'll find that the boys are more scared of a big smash-up that they'll live through. We reckon it's better to be killed than maimed.

'There's a bloke up at Park Royal Hospital that had a crash up the Woods [Borehamwood]. He's lost one arm, one leg and his sanity. It's better to be killed than have that happen.

'A smash-up can be expensive as well. A new bike can cost up to £400. Then there is insurance. This jacket cost ten quid, the crash helmet five. And the boots usually cost over £5.

'I get £7 a week. I pay £2.10s each week on the bike, and £2 to my mother for rent. The rest goes on petrol and cigarettes. It's not as though we can afford to be reckless.

'There are some characters who have done more than others and we respect them for it. But they are the characters to be beaten.

'There's an iron bridge on a bend near here. Someone goes round there at 80. Someone else tries to get round there faster. There's been about two dozen blokes killed there over the past few years.

'If you hit those iron girders, that's it. Hit them and you come out the other side like chips.'

'Couple of weeks ago, I pulled out from the Ace with a mate. I was hammering away in front of him, when my tax disc came off. I stopped and got off to fetch it, leaving the bike on the side stand. I couldn't find the disc and my mate was waiting, so I started up and hammered away. I went round the right-hand bend, up to the traffic lights and then started tanking it. I was doing about 85 to 90 as I came up to the left-hand bend. I went to crank it over but it wouldn't go. I'd left the stand down, you see. With the stand down I couldn't get round the bend.

The article featured a group of bikers underneath the railway arch. Jenny — the original 'girl on a motorcycle' — is on her Tiger Cub with its cow-horn handlebars next to her then-current boyfriend Steve Hammond. For 'Mary' in this article, read Jenny. 'I always gave a false name and age if I was interviewed in case my mum found out and when she saw this issue of _Today_ she went spare. "George" in the article was really my future husband Ron Wittich (see pages 174-175).'

'I put the brakes on, but I was heading straight for the girders. I thought: Blimey, I've bought it! But I was lucky. As the front wheel touched the kerb, I swung the bike round and scraped to a stop.'

The slang words of motorcycling are colourful, but easy to understand.

Hammering it means going fast. _Tanking_ it is lying flat on the machine at speed. _Dropping a cog_ is changing gear, and _cranking_ it _over_ means laying the bike over at a bend. There are others: _bombing it_ — going fast; _jazzing it_ — larking about in traffic; _grounding it_ — scraping; _clip-ons_ — drop handlebars. _Noddy men_ and _chicken-chasers_ are the police on two-stroke bikes.

Most motorcyclists have had at least one accident. Jeannette told me: 'The first thing I think of after an accident is that I'm alive. I had 44 stitches in my leg once and my foot was broken. I didn't feel any pain after the smash, I was too shocked. I just thought: I'm alive!'

'The first thing the boys ask,' said Speedy, 'is if their bike is all right.'

It was getting late. The café was packed when I left about midnight. The jukebox played. A boy was gazing at the wall, crash-helmet in his hand, reading the letter from a broken-hearted mother.

'Look, said Speedy, 'you've heard a lot tonight. Don't make it sound bad for us. Just tell the truth. How bad's that!'

Yes, how bad?

Today, January 14, 1961

Evening all ... Y'know, if I've got a bee in my bonnet about one particular thing, I suppose it's Road Safety — and you find most coppers are the same. It's not only the tragic side of the accidents that gets you down: it's the thoughtlessness, the selfishness, the sheer perishing lunacy — for sometimes it's nothing more nor less, believe me ... I was up at the Coroner's Court at the Town Hall the other day. There'd been a nasty pile-up on the bypass, and I had to go along with young Jamie, as a police witness ...

PC GEORGE DIXON, JANUARY 14, 1961

Then, that Saturday evening, episode 16 of the popular television series *Dixon of Dock Green* starring Jack Warner was broadcast titled 'The Burn-up'.

CAST LIST

PC George Dixon — Jack Warner
Sergeant Flint — Arthur Rigby
Andy Crawford C.I.D. — Peter Byrne
Sgt. Grace Millard — Moira Mannion
PC Lauderdale — Geoffrey Adams
Cadet Jamie Macpherson — David Webster
Det. Con. Hughes — Graham Ashley
WPC Kay Shaw — Jocelyne Rhodes
Coroner — Ivan Samson
Mike Jarrod — Jess Conrad
Dave 'Cha-Cha' Charlton — Melvyn Hayes
Alma — Lorna Henderson
Jean — Jill Tracey
Mr. Wilson — Rex Dyer
Mrs. Wilson — Dorothy Rose Gribble
Sid Jacobs — Harold Berens
Lorry driver — Patrick Connor
Doreen Burke — Valerie Stillwell
Jennie — Hilda Fenemore
Sister — Elizabeth Broom
4 Boys — Alan Lake, Del Ward
2 Girls — Jackie Pearlman, Jill Culpin
Ancient — Aubrey Danvers Walker

'It really started at the Ace caff on the bypass,' said Mike (Jess Conrad). 'Jimmy said let's have a burn-up ... Jimmy, me and Cha-Cha (Melvyn Hayes) and the three girls.' After Jimmy gets killed, we see first Mike at the inquest where the verdict is accidental death. Then, later in the station office, Dixon is in conversation with the desk sergeant: 'Coffee-bar cowboys. These young 'erbs who hang out at the caffs with their flash bikes and their girls. What's their local caff, Andy?' 'The "Ace"'. Dixon: 'That's the place. Might be an idea to pop up there sometime, and see what goes on.'

SCENE 2: CORONER'S COURT (DAY)

MIKE: We, we have this burn-up. Jimmy's up in front, on this big double-knocker he's just got —

CORONER: Double-knocker?

MIKE: Twin-cylinder. Well, we knock up seventy coming down from the Ace then we have to ease off for the roundabout.

CORONER: At what speed did you go over the roundabout?

MIKE: Oh — 45, 50.

CORONER: You mean it is possible for a motorcycle — with pillion passengers — to cross a roundabout at nearly 50 miles an hour?

MIKE: Sure, yes — if you gotta good bike, and the girl knows her stuff. You put the bike hard over, see — right down. Course, you might scrape a foot-rest, but not if you have 'em real high, racing position —

CORONER: *(Frowning)* Yes, yes. Go on.

MIKE: Well, we're over the roundabout, then down the straight, touching ninety. I think Jimmy was trying for the ton —

CORONER: 'The ton?' You mean a hundred miles an hour, don't you?

MIKE: That's right, sir. Well, there's this big car in front. Jimmy's just going to pass, then — bonk! The bloke claps on his anchors — the lot. I saw Jimmy swerve, but — well — no good. I braked, and pulled the bike over, to miss Jimmy. Course, we skidded, and took a tumble.

CORONER: And that's all?

MIKE: Yes, sir. That's all.

CORONER: The police officer has said that neither you nor the other motorcyclists wore crash-helmets. Is that a regular practice of yours?

MIKE: Well, yes, sir. The girls think they look a bit dippy in 'em, y'see and me — well you've got to hear your engine, haven't you?

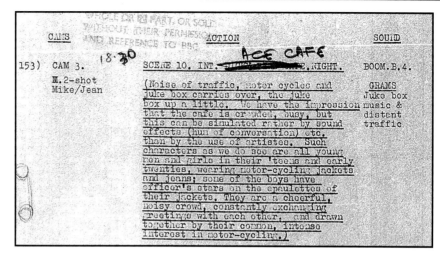

Unfortunately the transmission copies of many of the *Dixon* programmes no longer exist and all that remains of 'The Burn-up' is a copy of the script. This episode featured the death of a 17-year-old inexperienced motorcyclist whose girlfriend (Doreen Burke) was seriously injured on a pillion. As with most filming, actual place names are usually changed to avoid any subsequent claim for damages and, although shooting was scheduled at the Ace, the name of the cafe in the script was originally given as the 'Dicky Bird'. However, as this extract shows, at some stage a decision was made to use the real name . . . and thus a legend was born.

CORONER: Surely that is quite audible, even with a crash-helmet?

MIKE: Ah, but there's what you call valve bounce, y'see. It's a funny noise your valves make, at peak revs. If you hear that, you've gotta ease off, you might blow up your motor.

CORONER: But why drive the machine at these high speeds?

MIKE: *(Puzzled)* Well — Well, I mean — it's a fast bike!

(The Coroner gives Mike a long look before replying)

CORONER: Let me ask you a question, Jarrod. After this appalling accident — now that you realise the dangers — will you and your friends still go racing your machines along the bypass, going nowhere at ninety miles an hour?

MIKE: I suppose so — I mean _ we're not breaking any law. It's rotten about Jimmy — he was a good bloke — and I'm dead sorry about his Mum and Dad *(makes a puzzled, vague gesture)* But — well that's the game, isn't it? I mean — he was just unlucky.

CORONER: And is that all your friend's death has taught you?

MIKE: Like I said, that's the game.

CORONER: But surely, on the grounds of personal safety alone —

MIKE: Well, if you go, you go. I mean, you can only die once, can't you? Well, can't you?

(There is a shocked murmer from the court, a sob from Mrs Wilson. The Coroner raises his hand: there is silence. Mike looks about him, rather helpless. He catches Wilson's stare. Wilson is saddened, angry)

CORONER: All right, Jarrod. Stand down.

SCENE 12: ACE CAFE (NIGHT)

(The cafe is not so busy as previously, it being early evening. The jukebox is silent. Mike, Jean, Cha-Cha and Alma are standing at one end of the counter, talking over soft drinks and cakes. Syd Jacobs is behind the counter)

CHA-CHA: We did a ton-ten again last night. Will this new bike of yours touch that?

MIKE: *(Enthusiastic)* Easy — easy. It's a smasher, mate! Honest, you've never rid anything like it.

CHA-CHA: Looks a big bike — even for a double-knocker.

MIKE: It's a seven-fifty. Alloy heads, high-lift cams, rev counter — it's a real potent bike.

JEAN: They guarentee a ton-fifteen. Mike got the catalogue once.

MIKE: And that's the *production* job! Once you start tuning . . .

CHA-CHA: But where'd you get the lob? You said you were skint!

MIKE: Well, I haven't bought it, exactly . . .

CHA-CHA: You ain't bought it? But how . . .

JEAN: Save it . . . *(a glance at Syd)*

MIKE: *(Lowering his voice)* We borrowed it, see . . . just for a quick burn-up.

ALMA: Borrowed it? You mean, you — you pinched it!

MIKE: We'll dump it later, I was going nutty, not having a bike. It's no good, I'll have to get the lob, somehow. *(finishes his drink)* Get up behind Cha — I'll show you what she does.

CHA-CHA: Okey-doke.

JEAN: Don't go far, Mike. I want another go. I want to see what it feels like to touch a ton-fifteen!

MIKE: Just up the roundabout and down the hill. Put a record on — see if we can get back before it ends.

But the main damage to the cafe's reputation came in Scene 12 where scriptwriter Ted Willis introduced the concept of racing a record playing on the jukebox. Since that episode of *Dixon* was broadcast, record racing has gone down in the folklore of the Ace, repeated time and time again by writers and journalists over the years. But, as Noddy and others have categorically stated, it never happened beforehand. Records in those days were far too short and the much greater thrill was racing your mates.

ALMA: Mmm! That's really moving!

(The boys cram on their caps, hurry out as they go)

CHA-CHA: Didn't go much on double-knockers, meself. Too much vibration.

MIKE: Not this one, boy. It's dead smooth . . . it's a dream.
(Jean puts a coin in the juke-box, and the record begins. A powerful twin-cylinder motorcycle is heard starting up outside, with much revving of the engine. The machine zooms away, the crackle of its exhaust diminishing)

> Y'know motorcycling's a fine sport — one of the best — but, like every other vehicle, a motorbike can maim and kill unless it's ridden with proper care. I know I beef about Road Safety, but . . . well, straight up, the roads these days are more like battlefields, sometimes. So whether it's a car, motorbike, or whatever it is — take care always, won't you. Your life — and other people's — is in your hands: it's as simple as that . . . Goodnight all. . .
>
> PC GEORGE DIXON, JANUARY 14, 1961

And just like Dan Matthews in the American *Highway Patrol* series of the 1950s always ended each programme with a homespun homily ('Leave blood at the Red Cross, not on the highway'), so George Dixon finished each episode with a friendly word of advice. (Incidentally, Broderick Crawford, who played Dan Matthews, was no stranger to British roads as he had served in the UK during the Second World War and was even present at Glenn Miller's first concert in England in July 1944.)

ON British roads today, the only vehicle carrying more dead people than the motor-cycle is a HEARSE.

They have not yet finished counting the people who were killed on motor-bikes last year.

But they HAVE counted up the dead and the maimed for 1959.

And these are the figures: <u>1,680 riders killed, 128,614 riders injured.</u>

Injured is a harmless-looking word. It means crippled. Or disfigured for life. Or losing a limb. Or being blinded.

This is something that is more likely to happen to motor-cyclists than to any other class of people in Britain.

For every five four-wheeled vehicles—cars, vans, lorries—there is only one two-wheeled vehicle —motor-bike, scooter or moped.

The Lure

But two-wheelers clock up nearly **HALF** the total number of road casualties.
● The lure of the motor-bike is **SPEED**.
● Speed brings **DEATH**.
● And death comes to the **YOUNG**.

For the youngsters, death is the first and the last adventure.

IMAGINE a fresh-faced boy on his sixteenth birthday. On that day he can go out and buy a provisional driving licence.

Only Luck

He can go from the licensing office and plonk £25 down on a motor-bike.

He can drive away with only a set of L-plates for company.

AND A TURN OF THE THROTTLE LATER HE CAN BE LYING DEAD WHILE HIS WHEELS SPIN AT ONE HUNDRED MILES AN HOUR.

Only luck can guide him home in one piece.

YOUTHS between the ages of nineteen and twenty own more powered two-wheelers than any other age group.

Therefore more of them die.

In 1959, **2,059** motor-cyclists in this age group were' killed or injured.

The total for all other road users in the same age group was **287**.

The Ministry of Transport—which has problems—calls this "the most acute problem of the lot."

Acute?

It's **TERRIFYING**.

Statistics are boring. But these statistics skid out and hit you in the face!

The tabloids quickly took up the story, the *Daily Mirror* sensationalising the increasing death toll of young motorcyclists in their 'shock issue' of February 9.

● The chances of a motor-cyclist being killed are nineteen times greater than a car driver's.

● There were 28 per cent. more deaths and serious injuries in 1959 than in 1958.

● The deaths for 1960, when they are all recorded, will be even higher. During the first ten months, deaths and serious accidents were 2.2 per cent up on 1959.

At 10 mph

Striking a telegraph pole at 10 m.p.h. will jolt a motorist and dent his car.

The same collision will hurl a motor-cyclist 15 ft from the saddle.

THE Minister of Transport, Mr Ernest Marples, is alarmed at the dangers of motor-cycling. He is acting to cut them down.

But Mr Marples can't stop speed-hungry youngsters burning up the road at a hundred miles an hour.

Only the man with the throttle in his hand can do that.

Either him—or sudden death.

DEATH IS THE THIRD BRAKE ON EVERY MOTORBIKE.

Daily Mirror, February 9, 1961

Although the *Mirror* tempered their editorial by including advice on safe motorcycling, the following day, Friday, February 10, things came to a head at the Ace as Tony Purbrick explains. 'The Ace boys knew our shift times at DT2 better than most of us and were aware that the North Circular Road was usually theirs from about 11.30 p.m. nightly, especially Friday and Saturday nights (or so they thought), when they were in active competition with the neighbouring group on DT6's ground at the Busy Bee on the A41 near Watford. One night, about two weeks after the *Dixon of Dock Green* episode in which they were involved was broadcast, the late shift was ready to book off when in came the coloured complaints car crewed by John 'JC' Cutts who was angry, to say the least, as a result of a brick being thrown at the car from someone in the crowd of hundreds in the Ace car park. Something had to be done, and it was, that night.' Forty years later Tony put pen to paper to compose this poem about that night.

THE ACE BOYS

The Ace Boys were renowned, they led us a dance,
Their downfall had started, and their riding not so advanced.
It started late one night with a brick thrown at our car,
Cuttsey was on the crew, the maddest I've seen him, by far.

He drove into DT2, about booking-off time, I think,
Blue complaints car and his red face, he made quite a stink,
'Be fair Guv,' said John, 'It's time to cure it once and for all,
It's been going too long, they're making us look fools.'

The late shift stayed on, volunteers every one.
Grab a solo, get ready, it's going to be fun.
Get rid of gauntlets, brown driving gloves will do.
Cover crash helmet badge with First Aid tape and glue.

Disguised solo riders headed for the Ace en bloc.
Surveyed the Circ, looked over the car park and really took stock.
Then out they came, thinking all T/Ps had gone home.
One then another, convinced they were King and on the throne.

The North Circ was theirs, to hell with everyone else,
Their race to the Iron Bridge was an experience in itself.
Unfortunately for them, we were in position, up sun.
Like Spitfires in the Big One, waiting for the enemy to run.

The patience paid off and the T/Ps peeled off . . . Tally Ho! was the call,
Into the mêlée they went, thick and fast, one and all.
Groups were halted, the singles as well,
Three tenths, what's that? Two tenths, one tenth — to Hell!

We've got you, you're mine, it really was a ball,
Process were completed, multi and singles for all.
To say the T/Ps cleaned up, an understatement you bet,
The Station Officer who received them hasn't recovered yet.

The big court day arrived, to Willesden we went,
T'was difficult to get in as the Press had been sent.
'Time to pay?' was oft heard said, but it fell on deaf ears,
'Sell your bike, pay your fine, be relieved of further fears.'

The operation was a success and the problem solved,
The papers had a field day and the headlines were bold.
The thanks of the many filtered down to the few.
Ron Askham, Johnny Cutts, to name but just two.

One wonders where they are now, those Ace Boys so bold,
A mortgage . . . wife . . . kids . . . and now forty years old.

TONY PURBRICK, EX-PC 896

After 50 years of continuous law enforcement service, which began in the Royal Military Police, Tony has now established his own police museum in his basement — complete with his own old Met uniform!

Above: That same year — 1961 — the Metropolitan Police purchased the Daimler SP 250 — more popularly referred to as the Dart. Although the 2½-litre sports car was normally introduced for general use — not specifically for combatting the cafe racers — it was nevertheless useful at night because motorcycles from the Traffic Unit were not allowed out after midnight. Here, Tony Purbrick (left) and John Hooper are pictured in Briar Crescent, Northolt, where they had gone to take a statement from a witness to a previous road traffic accident. *Right:* A Honda Civic takes up the same parking space 40 years later outside No. 50. Tony was head-hunted by the world famous Pinkerton Detective Agency and he emigrated to the United States and was eventually promoted to Vice President and Director of International Operations. He also carried the dual title of managing director of all Pinkerton's European companies. He retired in 1991 and went on to security consulting operations for large shipping companies including Cunard.

THREE GIRLS AND 18 YOUTHS IN COURT

A POLICE swoop on a large crowd of motor cyclists gathered in the forecourt of the Ace Cafe, North Circular Road, Willesden, on Friday was described at Willesden Court on Monday when 18 youths and three girls appeared on charges of using insulting behaviour.

Many of the youths appeared in court wearing leather jackets and other motor cycling gear and a line of high-powered motor cycles stood by the kerb outside the court.

Of the 21 accused, one youth and three girls, all juveniles, were remanded to the juvenile court on bail until February 22. No evidence was given against them.

Of the remainder, six who asked for an adjournment to be legally represented and to call witnesses, were remanded for a week on bail.

They were: Norman Stanley New, aged 18, mechanic, of Gresley Road, Whitehall Park, N.19; Royston Stanley Joyce, aged 18, printer's engineer, of Scottswood Close, Bushey, Herts.; Brian Frederick Reid, aged 19, apprentice printer, of Scottswood Close, Bushey, Herts.; John Weenen, aged 19, fitter, of Canonbury Road, Enfield, Middlesex; Alan Kenneth Newman, aged 17, lathe operator, of White Wells Park, Enfield, Middlesex; Nigel Alistair Raeburn Cole, aged 17, clerk, of Friern Barnett Lane, Whetstone.

The remaining eleven all pleaded not guilty and three of them were cleared of the charge.

They were: Brian Edwin John Austin, aged 19, assistant sales manager, of Carlton House, Canter, Te

dressed in motor cycling gear were in the forecourt and sitting on the wall with their feet on the pavement.

"Some were indulging in horseplay while others were encouraging them," said one of the officers, P.c. Raymond Attewell.

Other officers stated that the youths were shouting and jostling each other, that some were jeering at passing motorists, and that people waiting at a bus stop appeared to be in fear.

£5 FINES

Fines of £6 were imposed on the eight, who were: Harry Martin, aged 18, labourer, of Gibbons Road, Kingston, Surrey; Timothy Burke, aged 17, mechanic, of Brooksmead Road, Sunbury - on - Thames, Middlesex; John Le Fort, aged 17, labourer, of Cross Road, Hornsey; Edward Charles Hutchins, aged 18, carpenter, of Kennington Drive, Sunbury-on-Thames; Kevin Patrick Brown, aged 17, machinist, of Lion Crescent, Sudbury-on-Thames; Noel Peter Doran, aged 17, mechanic, of Canbury Park Road, Kingston-on-Thames; John Bowpitt, aged 17, labourer, of Canbury Park Road, Kingston-on-Thames; and David William Angel, aged 19, farm labourer, of Nursery Road, Sunbury.

TWO YOUTHS ACCUSED OF TAKING AWAY CAR

TWO Willesden youths were committed in custody for sentence to London Sessions when they appeared on remand at Clerkenwell Magistrates' Court on Wednesday.

Barry Goodes, aged 19, wireman, of Melville Road, and Michael Patrick Collins, aged 19, car mechanic, of the same address, pleaded guilty the previous week at the court to taking and driving away a car and using it without being insured.

Goodes also pleaded guilty to driving without a licence and driving while disqualified.

STOPPED BY POLICE

The magistrate, Mr. T. F. Davis, told them: "We will let the Sessions see whether you ought to be sent to Borstal."

When the case was heard on February 8, the court was told that police on motor patrol stopped the two youths on the Great West Road at 1.15 a.m. that day. They admitted that the car they were driving was one they had taken without consent two hours earlier from Adelaide Road, Hampstead.

Stabbed wom

hin

A DEBATE rival more than 1 last week.

Youth mixed in age, tion given Mr East Willesde and the Left

The meeting w Willesden branch Nations Associatio chairmanship of Landy. Speaker Skeet, Mr. Laurie our M.P. for Wes Mr. Geoffrey W and Dr. Paul M Imperial College

FEAT

After outlining of disarmamen war, Mr. Willi the features of gramme for phas ral disarmament

Mr. Pavitt, wh for unilateral said its purpose w confidence in the nunciation was to an internatio

He said there nuclear weapons the world ten tim day only three the H-bomb.

Ready to ride away after the court hearing.

A police swoop on a large crowd of motorcyclists gathered in the forecourt of the Ace Cafe, North Circular Road, Willesden, on Friday was described at Willesden Court on Monday when 18 youths and three girls appeared on charges of using insulting behaviour.

Many of the youths appeared in court wearing leather jackets and other motorcycling gear and a line of high-powered motorcycles stood by the kerb outside the court.

A number of police officers, giving evidence, said they went to the cafe in three police cars and a police van in response to an emergency call.

The operation by DT2 resulted in a large number of arrests, all of whom appeared in due course at Willesden Court in St Mary's Road which had just been refurbished.

They stated that a crowd of about 100 youths and girls dressed in motorcycling gear were in the forecourt and sitting on the wall with their feet on the pavement.

'Some were indulging in horseplay while others were encouraging them,' said one of the officers, PC Raymond Attewell.

Other officers stated that the youths were shouting and jostling each other, that some were jeering at passing motorists, and that people waiting at a bus stop appeared to be in fear.

The first of them, Harry Martin, agreed in evidence that a crowd of about 100 had gathered in the forecourt of the cafe and he said, 'You've got to make a spectacular entry to the Ace.'

Martin said, 'We were all arrested for the simple reason that we were wearing leather jackets. We go down to the Ace to look at the bikes — people go in the cafe and leave their bikes to be seen.'

Willesden Chronicle, February 17, 1961

POLICE MOVE TO CHECK 'DEATH RIDES'

SPECIAL SITTINGS FOR MOTOR CYCLE SUMMONSES

Ace cafe juveniles in court

The death of another motorcyclist at Willesden the following week only served to fan the flames of the on-going police clamp-down on speeding on the North Circular — as highlighted in the headlines of the local newspapers.

A motorcyclist's pillion passenger was killed in an accident in Willesden Lane, Willesden Green, on Sunday.

He was 17-year-old Stanley Roy Barton, of Chapter Road, Willesden Green. The motorcycle was ridden by Barry Finch, 18, of Grampian Gardens, Hendon.

At traffic lights at the junction of Willesden Lane and Sidmouth Road, the machine was involved in a collision with a car driven by Mrs. Beatrice Sheffrin, of Donnington Road, Willesden.

Willesden Citizen, February 24, 1961

Motorcyclists who use the North Circular Road are in the news again. Following special watch by police patrols, more than 250 cases of alleged speeding have been reported in recent weeks.

Summonses are being issued and it is likely that special sittings of Willesden magistrates will be arranged to hear the cases. They will probably be dealt with in batches, beginning in the middle of next month.

Never before have so many motorcyclists using one stretch of road been prosecuted in such a short period.

The four-mile stretch on which it is alleged the offences have been committed runs right through the borough of Willesden from Hanger Lane to Staples Corner.

It was only on February 10 that 20 police officers in three police cars and a police van swooped on a crowd of 100 motorcyclists and their girl friends at Stonebridge. They made 21 arrests for the alleged use of insulting behaviour. Some of the youths were subsequently fined £5.

Now the 18 to 22-year-olds, who are being summoned, are, it is believed, holding meetings to decide on their defence.

It is understood that some defendants will answer more than one summons alleging the same offence on different dates and it is also believed that many of the cases will be based on 'index plate' evidence.

When the charges of alleged insulting behaviour were heard at Willesden Court, one of the youths who gave evidence said:

'We were arrested for the simple reason that we were wearing leather jackets. We go down there to look at the bikes — people leave their bikes to be seen.'

Always a favourite rendezvous for motorcyclists, the North Circular Road jumped into the limelight when it was featured in a recent television programme a few weeks ago and since then it has attracted youths from a still wider area. They meet in the vicinity, talk 'shop' and inspect each other's motorcycles.

Willesden Chronicle, February 24, 1961

Six youths who were among a crowd of leather-jacketed motorcyclists arrested in a police swoop on the car park of the Ace Cafe, North Circular Road, Willesden, on February 10, all pleaded not guilty at Willesden Court on Monday to a charge of using insulting behaviour. In all 18 youths and three girls were arrested.

Willesden Chronicle, February 24, 1961

NINETY-FOUR MOTOR CYCLISTS ARE FINED

Four more fined after Ace Cafe car ark swoop

YOUTHS IN LEATHER JACKETS CHARGED

YEAR'S DRIVING BAN FOR MOTOR CYCLISTS
TOOK BEND AT 75 m.p.h.

BOUGHT DUTY FREE LIQUOR

FOUR teenage motor cyclists, said at Willesden Court on Thursday last week to have drawn away from a police patrolman whose speedometer was registering 75 m.p.h. on the North Circular Road, Willesden, were each fined £20 and disqualified from driving for twelve months on summonses for dangerous ...

FIRM THAT NEVER MAKES A PROFIT
But provides

Police have taken up the battle against speed-crazy motorcyclists and their young girlfriends who's activities alarm the residents of the North Circular Road area. Every evening and at weekends these youngsters aged between 18 and 22, keep local residents on edge as they roar up and down the curved stretches of the road between Stonebridge and Neasden. Their objective is to race on this 40 miles an hour limited highway, in many cases, at speeds in excess of a 'Ton' (100 m.p.h.).

The police are trying to bring these 'death rides' to an end, and within the next few weeks 100 motorcyclists are to appear before Willesden magistrates for alleged speeding offences. In all, more than 250 summonses are being issued.

For many years residents of the area have been campaigning to end the race-track-like activities of youngsters using this stretch of road.

When seven people were killed in two months on this 'black' stretch of road, the Braincroft Residents Association organised protest demonstrations — and traffic lights were erected. However, it is apparent that these have done little to curb the speed addicts who wear black denim trousers and motorcycle jackets.

Police have been keeping close observation on the youths and their activities. The summonses for speeding follow a police swoop in the area on February 10 when several youngsters were arrested and charged with insulting behaviour.

There is a general feeling among the motorcyclists in the North Circular Road area that they are being victimised because they wear black leather jackets and as a result are placed in a disreputable category.

But, the police believe that due to the extensive publicity the area has been given many more motorcyclists from as far afield as Southend and other coastal and provincial towns epitomise Stonebridge as a sort of TT race track.

Mr. Ben Wishlade, Willesden's road safety officer is 'alarmed' at the situation and unnecessary waste of life.

'The problem is an old one' he said 'but TV programmes and other publicity has brought it to public light. It has been well known that these motorcyclists congregate in the cafes.

'They put on a long playing record or a short one and try to get to some point and back before the record finishes.'

Mr. Wishlade thinks that with the introduction of the 40 m.p.h limit much of the flagrant speeding has slackened off, but the problem still exists.

The British Safety Council also condemn the 'do a ton boys'.

Mr. Leonard D. Hodge, the National Director of the Council, says that the only way to counter the 'Glorious Death Cult' that seems to be growing up, is to play down the glory of speed and spills, and play up the sordid, undignified side — the discrippled cripples, the month in hospital, the artificial limbs that result from the activities of the 'do a ton boys.'

'If only these mad-cap motorcyclists could once see one of their friends crying or being sick in an ambulance on his way to the operating theatre, he would soon forget the thrill of speeding,' he said.

West London Star, March 4, 1961

Fines totalling over £800 were imposed at a special court at Willesden on Friday, on 94 motorcyclists convicted of speeding. Many of the offences were committed in North Circular Road.

A large force of police officers explained that police vehicles, without official markings, followed offenders and checked their speeds 'over 3/10ths of a mile'. Two officers said action followed 'complaints.'

One youth was alleged to have told an officer that the police were having a purge. Several youths who disagreed with police evidence declined to give evidence themselves on the ground that it was 'no use.'

Apart from one penalty of £3 the fines ranged from £5 to £15. Some of the alleged speeds were in the region of 70 miles an hour.

At Willesden Court, on Monday, the regular traffic offences day, the offenders dealt with were mainly motorists. The majority of fines were £3 and £5, with a maximum of £8 for a speed of 65-70 m.p.h.

It is believed that about another 200 motorcyclists have been summoned for speeding.

Willesden Chronicle, March 24, 1961

The Iron Bridge featured in the description of one chase by Tony Purbrick's colleague, PC Ronald Jamieson.

Four teenage motorcyclists, said at Willesden Court on Thursday last week to have drawn away from a police patrolman whose speedometer was registering 75 m.p.h. on the North Circular Road, Willesden, were each fined £20 and disqualified from driving for 12 months on summonses for dangerous speed.

They were: Keith Edward Batley, aged 18, printer, of Broad Walk, Winchmore Hill; Peter Terence Field, aged 19, driver-salesman, of Haggerston Road, E.8; Terence Ernest Bewg, aged 18, apprentice motor mechanic, of Isledon Road, King's Cross; and Michael John Gibbons, aged 18, apprentice motor mechanic, of Wilmot Street, Bethnal Green.

All four pleaded not guilty to summonses for dangerous speed but they all pleaded guilty to summonses for exceeding the 40 m.p.h. speed limit.

Police Constable Ronald Jamieson said that at 9.50 p.m. on February 6 he was engaged on special patrol duty on the North Circular Road, keeping observation on motorcyclists. He saw the four defendants and another motorcyclist travelling towards Hendon at a fast speed and followed them.

At the junction of St. Raphael's Way the police speedometer was recording 60 m.p.h. and the group increased their speed until the police speedometer showed 75 m.p.h.

'At that time they were still pulling away from me,' he said.

PC Jamieson continued that on approaching the Iron Bridge at Neasden, the motorcyclists overtook another vehicle and on the bend, which was very acute, they overtook two other motor cars.

'Their speed was so great — in excess of 75 m.p.h. round this bend — that one of the machines was banked over so far in order to negotiate the bend and not collide with the centre safety fence that sparks were seen coming from the footrest or some part of the nearside,' he said.

On reaching the traffic lights at Neasden, the group of motorcyclists pulled up — the lights were red. Then the bell of a police car began to ring from behind. Batley and Bewg looked round, saw the police car and edged forward to take up a position between two vehicles in front. When the lights changed, they accelerated rapidly away.

PC Jamieson said he went after them, overtaking them and stopping them. Both made no reply when the offences were pointed out. The other two motorcyclists were stopped by other officers.

Answering Batley, who asked, 'You had a faster machine than ours, why were we pulling away from you?' PC Jamieson said, 'The machine I was riding was capable of speeds in excess of 75 m.p.h. but that was quite fast enough as far as I was concerned.'

Batley told the court, 'We started from the Ace Cafe and we did not exceed 65 m.p.h. I changed down going round the bridge.'

Field and Bewg also stated that they did not exceed 65 m.p.h. and Bewg added, 'I had full control of my machine'.

Gibbons said he agreed with his friends and added, 'It would be impossible to go round the Iron Bridge bend at 75 m.p.h.'

Answering the chairman, Mr. C. H. Amies, Batley, Field and Bewg said they were buying their motorcycles on hire purchase.

The four of them were granted an absolute discharge on the summons for exceeding 40 m.p.h. on payment of 4s costs in each case.

Willesden Chronicle, March 31, 1961

The infamous bridge looks still much as it did 40 years ago.

Some of those summoned pleaded guilty by post and the mitigating circumstances make humorous reading. One boy wrote that he had only just bought his 1,000 c.c. machine. He had since found out it was so powerful that he did not realise his speed. He had now sold it. Another said his was an ex-police machine and was so quiet that its speed was deceiving. A letter saying,'My thoughts were on my fiancèe,' drew from the magistrate the comment: 'I hope she is thinking of him now. Fined £10.' A similar fine was imposed on a National Serviceman who wrote that he had just got married and was returning to camp. 'I am afraid my mind was more on my wife than on the speed limit.' Speeding home after attending Willesden Technical College because he was hungry cost another youth £7. A rider who wrote that it would never happen again blamed his speed of 50 m.p.h. on a 'strong following wind!' Two men claiming to be members of a motorcycle club in Tottenham wrote to dissociate themselves from Ace Cafe motorcyclists. *Above:* **Then and now outside the Ace.**

More than 350 motorcyclists have been reported for speeding on the North Circular Road, Willesden, and the surrounding area since January and now that more than 150 have been fined at the local court — some have also been disqualified from driving — the word has gone round. 'Watch out for the Law when you're over that way.'

Of the motorcyclists who have appeared in court so far, the vast majority are black-jacketed youths coming from all over London and the provinces and many have said that they were on their way to their favourite rendezvous, the Ace Cafe at Stonebridge, when they found police patrols on their tails.

Fines ranging from £7 to £20 were imposed at Willesden on motorcyclists for offences such as speeding, carrying an unauthorised passenger, and failing to display L plates. Of the 63 motorcyclists summoned, 37 pleaded guilty by letter and the rest made Court appearances. Fines totalling nearly £700 were imposed.

A schoolteacher motorcyclist, George Cherry, of Farm Way, Worcester Park, Surrey, alleged to have done 50-55 m.p.h. on the North Circular Road on January 29, wrote to the court:-

'Unfortunately of late, the good name of the motorcycling fraternity as a whole has suffered from an excessive amount of publicity which the most popular of the popular Press has been giving to the least responsible members of the motorcycling movement.

'I refer, of course, to the young, inexperienced riders who seem intent on turning the public highway into a race track. I do not wish to be associated with this kind of behaviour. I am a rider of some experience — about 95,000 miles over the last six or seven years.'

Mr. Cherry was fined £5 for speeding and £2 for driving without a driving licence.

Willesden Chronicle, March 31, 1961

'We started putting on special patrols to catch them. One system we used was for two of us to wait past the Harrow Road junction and, when we saw them roaring down, we would pull them in and book them for exceeding the speed limit. They had it in their minds that we had to follow them for 3/10ths of a mile but in fact we didn't have to follow them at all because two experienced traffic officers could say from their experience that they were way above the speed limit and put them in the book. If we were out on the motorcycles we would wait out of sight. You would get blokes lining up at the lights just like Wembley speedway, waiting for the tapes to go up. We would tuck in behind them and either try to go through the lights with them or hang back if they turned red. When they got the green we were away with them but there were times when I thought to myself: What am I doing chasing these silly sods at 75 m.p.h. If something goes wrong . . . so if it was getting a bit lairy I would back off and just get an index plate. You could usually only remember one number until you stopped to write it down.'

Ron Jamieson (right) about to leave DT2 on patrol. With him are PC Eric 'Ginger' Lowen (left) and Harold Milner. 'I was stationed at DT2 (see page 73),' explains Ron, 'from 1949 until it moved to new premises in Athlon Road, Alperton, in 1970. We parked underneath, behind Wembley police station on the corner, our entrance being in Ranelagh Road *(above)*. The workshop was located up a ramp from Harrow Road which led into the top floor where the cars and motorcycles were serviced. One of our duties was to escort unusual or large loads and, if the route went past the Ace, the driver would most likely want to pull into the layby and go in the cafe for a cup of tea. We would join them but there were always some motorcyclists there so it was a bit like going into the lion's den. If we saw riders just wearing a shirt we knew they were not ardent motorcyclists because if they came off their arms would be ripped to shreds. We called them 'shirtsleevers'. They used to line up across the road at the Harrow traffic lights, waiting for the green, then they were off.

Forty years on, Ron returns to DT2, the site of the former police garage now occupied by a block of flats.

UP, UP, UP WENT THE SPEEDOMETER

THE television programme, "Dixon of Dock Green" was referred to by Mr. George Shindler at Willesden Court on Thursday, last week, when he prosecuted a 19-year-old motor-cyclist alleged to have drawn away from a police car travelling at 80 m.p.h. on the North Circular Road, Willesden.

"It is, perhaps significant that on that particular night there was this programme on television which dealt with speeding youngsters on motor cycles at the Ace Café. Whether that has any bearing on the case I'm not prepared to say," commented Mr. Shindler.

Against the motor cyclist, Barry John Cheese, of Fowell Street, Notting Hill, were seven away from it," added Mr. Shindler.

He said that near the junction with Park Avenue, a car was signalling that it was turning across the road. The motor cyclist did not reduce speed, but squeezed between the car and the centre lane. The speedometer was still reading 80 m.p.h. at this time.

At Western Avenue and Hanger Lane, the motor cyclist ignored traffic signals, accelerated away and was "lost".

He was seen the following

Noddy got his comeuppance in January 1961 and three months later he was in the dock for his own tussle with Ron Jamieson. What is interesting is that by now the *Dixon* episode was being openly cited as a bad influence and Barry was specifically asked by the magistrate if he had watched the programme. Well had he? 'Of course I saw it', Barry told us!

The television programme, *Dixon of Dock Green* was referred to by Mr. George Shindler at Willesden Court on Thursday, last week, when he prosecuted a 19-year-old motorcyclist alleged to have drawn away from a police car travelling at 80 m.p.h. on the North Circular Road, Willesden.

'It is, perhaps significant that on that particular night there was this programme on television which dealt with speeding youngsters on motorcycles at the Ace Cafe. Whether that has any bearing on the case I'm not prepared to say,' commented Mr. Shindler.

Against the motorcyclist, Barry John Cheese, of Fowell Street, Notting Hill, were seven summonses alleging dangerous and careless driving, dangerous speed, exceeding 40 m.p.h. on the North Circular Road, failing to stop when directed to do so by police, and failing to conform to traffic signals, all on January 15.

Mr. Shindler told the bench that just after midnight on January 15, Cheese was followed from Durand Way, Willesden, to the Ace Cafe by the police car and a speed of 55 m.p.h. was recorded. When he turned across the intersection, the police car pulled alongside, its bell was rung and Cheese was directed to pull to the side of the road.

'Instead he accelerated away back in the direction from which he had come,' continued Mr. Shindler.

He said the police car followed and by Willesden Council's depot the police speedometer recorded 60 m.p.h. At Heather Park Drive, Cheese turned right again and accelerated back towards Ealing. Again he was followed and by the time they reached Iveagh Avenue, the speedometer was recording 70 m.p.h.

'Although the motor car increased its speed to 80 m.p.h., the motorcycle still pulled away from it,' added Mr. Shindler.

He said that near the junction with Park Avenue, a car was signalling that it was turning across the road. The motorcyclist did not reduce speed, but squeezed between the car and the centre lane. The speedometer was still reading 80 m.p.h. at this time. At Western Avenue and Hanger Lane, the motorcyclist ignored traffic signals accelerated away and was 'lost'.

Cheese was seen the following day and the officer immediately recognised him, but Cheese denied that he was the rider of the motorcycle.

PC Ronald Jamieson said in evidence that he definitely identified Cheese as the motorcyclist. He agreed that he might have told Cheese afterwards, 'It was an act of God that you were not killed.'

Cheese, on oath, said he was at home on the evening of January 14 and went to bed about 11 p.m. or 11.15 p.m. He did not get up until the following morning. Cross-examined, he agreed that he watched television on Saturday night, but he did not see a programme called *Dixon of Dock Green*. He remembered hearing about it. Mr. Shindler: 'Did that programme encourage you to go out on your motorcycle?' — 'No sir.'

Mrs. Ivy Cheese, also of Fowell Street, Notting Hill, said her son went to bed about 11 p.m. and did not go out until the following day.

Cheese was found guilty on six summonses and fined a total of £35. He was also ordered to pay £3 3s. costs. His licence was endorsed.

Willesden Chronicle, April 14, 1961

'It was specially dangerous following shirtsleevers if there were four or five of them,' explains Ron, 'because if one of them went down, he might bring down the rest, particularly at the Iron Bridge where they did not always line up properly to take the bend and often ran out of road. The boys thought it was all a joke but it didn't worry us as we were putting them in the book. I must have booked dozens and dozens of them although I never had to arrest anyone just for speeding. I did get a bit of lip like 'You can't do this!' or 'You've not followed me!' but it was largely good-natured and I would just reply: 'Righto, Fred, see you in court.' The motorcyclists were not only reported for excessive speed. Depending on the circumstances, some were reported for reckless, careless or dangerous driving which usually carried a period of disqualification. In addition, when stopped, all the machines were examined and many were reported for defective brakes. It was also not unusual to discover that there was no insurance in force. There were no cautions; everyone went to court and I was always there. We knew we had to crack the problem because otherwise they would be the winners. It wasn't just 'them or us'; it was for the other people using the road. One boy said that I had chased him all over London but we never targeted one motorcycle. You might book someone in one area and then see him elsewhere exceeding the limit so would book him again because you knew the bloke was a definite speedster. When it started at first it was them or us but then it got a bit tedious. It mainly took place in the evenings but we were neglecting other areas merely to kill this Ace Cafe-North Circular problem. One Friday night, I went down to the cafe with a colleague, Reg Leah, to see if we could sort them out once and for all. We replaced our white gauntlets with black driving gloves and covered the badge on our Corker crash-helmets. In February 1961, we commenced special patrols in the area and over a period dozens of riders were reported. They all had to attend Willesden Court on the same day, after which we had no further problems. I think they got the message!'
Top: A contingent from DT2 about to depart for the Queen's Review Police Parade in Hyde Park in July 1954 when 10,000 officers marched ten abreast before Her Majesty. L-R: Bill Coles, Eric Disney, Noel Westmoreland, Ron Jamieson and Harry Brown.

And in January 2002, 41 years after he was booked by Ron, Barry met him again . . . and even stood in the old dock in Willesden Magistrates Court, now derelict and abandoned to the local feathered population!

But for some of the lads this only served to add a little more excitement and so the chases continued throughout 1961 — not that we are saying that Wally and Charlie seen here chatting up the girls, were in anyway involved!

Caught speeding on his motorcycle twice within three days, George Peter Tate, of Cranleigh-gardens, Kenton, was fined a total of £10 at Harrow Court on Friday. He wrote pleading guilty, but made no comment about the offences.

Police Sergeant A. Cannon told the magistrates, police saw Tate speeding in Kenton Road on April 29, and on that occasion his speed was from 50 to 55 miles an hour. On May 2 he was seen in Charlton Road, Kenton, and his speed varied from 44 to 48 miles an hour.

The Observer and Gazette, June 15, 1961

The 'antics' of a 17-year-old Stonebridge, Willesden youth on The Promenade, Leysdown, Kent, one evening in July caused some considerable interest to holiday-makers there, magistrates at Sheerness were told on Monday.

The youth, John William Peters, of Brett Road, Stonebridge, drove his motorcycle combination round a road island at least 21 times, Mr. M. Lewer, prosecuting, said.

Peters, who denied riding the machine without reasonable consideration, was found guilty and fined £3.

Willesden Chronicle, September 15, 1961

A 65 m.p.h. chase through Harrow was described at Harrow Court on Friday when a young Greenford man was summoned for speeding dangerously in Pinner Road on July 22. Michael George Freeth, of Bingley Road, pleaded not guilty to speeding dangerously, but guilty to exceeding the speed limit.

He was found guilty on the first summons and fined £30 with a year's disqualification, and ordered to pay £1 1s costs.

On his own behalf Freeth said that he had gone fast because he wanted to get his girl friend home before 10.30 p.m..

Police Constable J. Mitchell said that a motorcycle with a female pillion passenger passed him in North Harrow at about 10.30 p.m. on July 22 going towards Harrow at a fast speed. He gave chase in his patrol car.

Over the half-mile of Pinner Road between Durham Road and Junction Road he followed at an even distance of 30 yards and speeds between 40-65 m.p.h. were recorded — most of the time they were driving at 65 m.p.h.

At the junction with Vaughan Road the motorcycle went to the right-hand side of the road to overtake two lines of traffic. The zebra crossing there was passed at high speed, when three people were about to cross. At two junctions on the left side further on, vehicles had to brake hard to avoid an accident. Near Oxford Road the motorcycle swung out hard to the wrong side of the road to take a sharp left-hand bend.

Freeth eventually slowed down to 40 m.p.h. at a bus stop just before Junction Road as a bus pulled up, said the officer. They started to gong the motorcyclist, who looked round several times. The chase continued over Roxborough Bridge and ended in Lascelles Avenue where for the police to stop him.

Freeth denied that he looked round 'several times.' He thought the bell was being rung by an ambulance. When he did Freeth slowed down sufficiently to look round he realized that he was being followed by a police car and slowed down.

PC Mitchell told the court that the car was not the usual type of patrol car as it had neither a 'police' sign nor loudspeakers. PC R. Harms, driver of the car, said that in front of Freeth had been another motorcyclist going at a fast speed and it appeared that Freeth was keeping company with him. This machine had gone down College Road and had been 'going too fast to be caught.'

The Observer Gazette, October 5, 1961

To say that the Ace Cafe, Stonebridge, had a bad reputation was 'putting it mildly,' a police officer said at Willesden Magistrates' Court on Monday. Four men who were alleged to have fought with plain-clothes police while being questioned outside the cafe on October 22 appeared at the resumed hearing.

The court was told that five police officers — one wearing a suede jacket and tight, black jeans, and another a cloth cap and muffler — noticed that the men had blood on their jackets, and two had blood on their hands, when they went into the cafe at 12.45 a.m. When the men came out 15 minutes later they were stopped for questioning. The officers said they were police and produced their warrant cards.

PC Mead said Burns told him: '— off. I don't care who you are.'

PC Elson showed his warrant card and Burns punched him in the stomach.

PC Mead said he went to help PC Elson and Burns kicked him in the legs. He pulled Burns' coat over his head and a hammer fell from his clothes.

The four were arrested and taken to the police station, where Burns punched PC Elson on the jaw and had to be restrained.

PC Mead said when he asked where the bloodstains came from, the accused said they had been 'punching trees.'

Counsel for Green asked: 'Has the Ace Cafe a bad reputation?' — 'That is putting it mildly'

'You expect trouble when you are round it?' — 'Yes, you never know what to expect.'

PC Elson was asked why the men were not stopped before going into the cafe. He said: 'This place is so full of disreputable types that if we had gone in it would have caused chaos.'

PC Robinson said he went to Arnold and something fell from his hand. He picked up a fixed-blade throwing knife. PC Robinson said he grabbed Arnold to stop him joining in a scuffle. Arnold swung round and punched him in the chest. PC Duffin said Green hit him on the neck with his hand and dropped a large file 'from his person.' He showed the file to Green, who said: 'That's not mine.'

PC Wetherill said Mitchell struck him in the chest and kicked him once on the knee.

Arnold told the court that they had come from a dance at the Abbey Hotel, Stonebridge. While there, a tray of glasses was knocked on to the carpet and he cut his hand picking up the pieces. They walked to the cafe and had a cup of coffee. Arnold said as he left the cafe a man approached him, and said, 'Where do you come from, John?' He replied, 'Hendon.'

Arnold said he stood his ground and the man held him by the lapels and produced a warrant card. He asked what it was all about, and the man said, 'Get in that car and you will find out.'

However, in November events at the Ace took a turn for the worse as the extracts show. Michael Robinson, an ex-PC stationed at Willesden Green, still recalls this incident when he was called to the cafe while an R/T operator on night duty. 'Someone was reportedly brandishing a knife and I remember dashing into the kitchen determined to beat all the others and the suspect dropping the knife when he saw me. Charlie Gridley, the driver, who I met coming into the kitchen as I was walking my prisoner out, commented later he'd never seen anyone nicked so fast!'

Arnold said he did not strike a blow or have a weapon. The bloodstains on his friends' clothes must have come from his hand. A knife was shown him at the police station, but it was not the one produced in court. He had said nothing to the police about trees.

Willesden Chronicle, November 10, 1961

A newspaper reporter once accused me of buying a motorbike and a leather jacket as a kind of gimmick to attract teenagers to my church. That is quite untrue. I had a motorbike long before leather jackets had become the rage. In fact, my outfit when I first started motorcycling would certainly raise a laugh among the young motorcyclists of today. It consisted of a green beret, long blue police mac, riding breeches and DR boots, all bought at the local surplus stores.

As for my bike — a BSA Bantam — I got it simply to get around my parish which at that time was in a new housing area near London Airport.

I was taught to ride by a member of our youth club, Eric Hall, who allowed me to practise on his brand-new Douglas Dragonfly. We used to go out in the late evening so that no one could see my escapades.

Eventually he decided that I was ready to take my test. I went to Ealing and failed. The examiner was a woman and I'm convinced that her pet aversions were vicars and motorbikes. In any event, not only did she fail me but, as if to twist the knife in the wound, she informed me that I was a menace to the public. Perhaps I was. But I passed next time — only just, for I ran out of petrol on the way home!

This stage in my motorcycling career could hardly be called successful. The bike was a dead loss. I can't remember how many times I pushed it from Hanworth to Twickenham for the dealer to tackle the latest fault. One day I was vainly kicking it outside the house of a parishioner. The milkman was chatting on the doorstep and remarked to the woman: 'What a pity vicars aren't allowed to swear.' Little did he know! Twice it broke down on the way to a wedding and I was so embarrassed at conducting marriage services with greasy hands that I decided to sell it and go back to my old push bike.

I was so completely fed up with motorcycles at this stage that I vowed I would never have another one. This resolve I kept until 1959 when the Bishop sent me to take charge of the Eton College Mission at Hackney Wick. This is a big and busy parish and it soon became clear that I must have some form of transport. Since I had never learned to drive a car I decided to take a chance and buy another bike. This time it was a secondhand C15 BSA. It was almost like starting to learn to ride all over again. I used to get up about 4 a.m. and ride around the empty streets.

It was at this point that influence on the situation came from a completely different direction — the church! Back in 1952 the Reverend William Shergold had purchased his first motorcycle to get round his extended parish of All Saints, Hanworth. When in 1959 he was posted to the other side of London to take charge of the Eton College Mission at Hackney, he bought another and so his reputation as the motorcycling vicar was born. Earlier that year, the curate, the Reverend John Oates, had formed a church youth club with the appropriate title the '59 Club' which had been opened by Cliff Richard on January 8. In his secondary role as Road Safety Officer of the North London branch of the Triumph Owners' Club, Reverend Shergold, (or Father Bill as he was affectionately referred to by the boys), was ever mindful of the death toll of young riders and wanted to help in a positive way.

The C15 was a dream after the Bantam, but I wasn't entirely certain that I had done the right thing in buying a bike. Perhaps it would have been more in keeping with the dignity of a middle-aged vicar to have bought a car and learned to drive. Then my mind was made up for me.

I remember the incident quite vividly. We were having lunch in the Clergy House when the phone rang. A little boy in our Sunday school had been playing in a bombed site and a huge piece of concrete had fallen on his head. He was badly hurt and his parents wanted a priest to visit him at once. I knew I

Astride his Speed Twin, Father Bill sets out from the Eton College Mission.

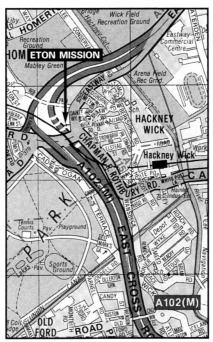

St Mary of Eton survived the building of the East Cross Route.

should have to use my bike. It sounded simple enough. But Brentwood was a long way from Hackney and it would mean going along the notoriously busy Eastern Avenue. There was no time for hesitation and I set off at once. It was a nightmare ride for one so inexperienced, but I got there and was able to pray with the little boy. Incidentally, he made a remarkable recovery.

Safely back at the Eton Mission, I was filled with a strange sense of elation. Not only had I conquered my fear of traffic, I had been able to use the bike for doing my work as a priest. Next morning in church I deliberately offered my bike to God and asked Him to make use of it in His work. It was a prayer which has been answered in a way I could never have dreamed of.

For the next two or three years I used the bike for pottering around my parish, but the thought never entered my head that one day I would start a club for motorcyclists. Most of my time was taken up with the youth club, which had just been launched by the Reverend John Oates.

By this time the motorcycle disease had really taken hold of me. I traded in my C15 for a 1959 Speed Twin and began to enjoy the thrills of a big bike. I even bought a crash helmet (police-style with peak) and a leather jacket (three-quarter length, of course). Then one day I read in the daily papers that a special service for motorcyclists had been held in the newly opened cathedral at Guildford. This struck me as odd because cathedrals tend to be rather respectable. But it gave me an idea.

If Guildford could do it, why couldn't Hackney Wick? Why couldn't we have a get-together at the Mission for motorcyclists in north and east London? For the first time in my life I wrote a letter to a paper asking if anyone would be interested in such a service and almost at once I got a letter from Bob Matthews, general secretary of the Triumph Owners' Club, saying he thought it was a good idea and would like to help me organize the event.

Rev. William Shergold, Link, 1966

Princess Margaret is to visit the '59 Club' run by Eton Mission at Hackney Wick, and one of the largest youth organisations in the country, on March 22. The Princess, who expects to be accompanied by the Bishop of Bath and Wells and, it is hoped, her husband, Lord Snowdon, requested that no special arrangements be made. She wants to see an ordinary club night in session.

Cliff Richard, pop-singer extraordinary, is president of the '59 Club' and the 900-member club is hoping he will put on a show for the royal visitor.

Press report, March 14, 1962

Princess Margaret and Lord Snowdon wowed the patrons when they made their first visit to an East End youth club swing session this week. The Princess, still recovering from an attack of laryngitis, led three clergymen and 700 delighted teenagers in a clapping, stamping accompaniment as the Shadows, Britain's top guitar group, twanged out one of their recent hits, *F.B.I.*

'Our 59 Club was immensely successful,' recalls Father Bill, 'and a most fabulous evening in the early days was when Princess Margaret and Lord Snowdon visited us. We had Mike Berry and the Outlaws providing the music with a very special guest star, Cliff Richard and the Shadows. Cliff brought his mother along — she is on the extreme right of the photo. My mother is just shaking hands with the Princess, The Reverend Oates is in the background.' By the time Cliff made his return visit there were over 900 members of the 59 Club . . . and Father Bill had plans to extend the membership in a most unusual direction.

Then, as uninhibited in the presence of Royalty as at their informal sessions, members of the 59 Club whistled and screamed their delight as their singing idol and club president, Cliff Richard, appeared on stage behind the smiling princess.

Unperturbed by the rowdy enthusiasm, Princess Margaret said to him, 'Please, you must sing for me *The Young Ones*.'

Cliff was also suffering from an attack of laryngitis — his doctor let him out of bed for the occasion — but it was not too bad to prevent his complying with a Royal command. Holding his throat, he sang two verses of the song, but left the high notes unsung. When Cliff apologised for his singing the Princess who was having her first day out after her own mild attack, told him: 'I understand.'

After the programme was over the Royal couple went on a tour of the club. They mingled with club members and had drinks at the milk bar, staying on long after their scheduled time of departure.

'The Princess . . . she was marvellous,' said Cliff Richard.

Sunday Times, March 25, 1962

Meanwhile plans were slowly taking shape for our big event which was now fixed for a Sunday in May 1962. We had roped in the local road safety officer and we sent out dozens of circulars to all the motorcycle clubs in the area. Then something happened which was to have a profound effect on the whole future course of events. One day, while I was talking about the service with some of the lads from the Triumph Owners', somebody said: 'Of course the people you really ought to invite to your service are those young hooligans who go blasting along the North Circular Road.'

'That's all very well,' said I, 'but I don't know any of them. How can I get in touch with them?'

'If you really want to meet them you should go along to the Ace Cafe.'

'Okay.' I said, 'I will!'

Until now we had thought only of inviting members of highly respectable motorcycle clubs to our service. The other section of the motorcycling fraternity was completely unknown to me.

I did recall, however, a magazine article I had read some years before whilst waiting to have my hair cut. It was the sort of article which appears from time to time in the American Press, describing the activities of the Hell's Angels. It was lavishly illustrated with pictures taken at the Ace. It certainly wasn't calculated to inspire confidence in anyone proposing to visit that cafe for the first time.

The more I thought about it the more alarmed I became. The time I chose for my trip to the Ace was a Sunday afternoon. Had I known more about the habits of young motorcyclists I certainly would not have chosen that particular time. The Ace is about 13 miles from Hackney Wick and I set out with several posters rolled up on the back of my bike, hoping that I might persuade the proprietors to put one up for me. Unsure of the kind of reception I should get, I wrapped a scarf round my neck covering up my dog-collar.

Just past Staples Corner about a dozen bikes ridden by sinister-looking figures in black leathers roared past in the opposite direction. I felt almost sick with fear. By the time I had passed under the bridges at Stonebridge Park I was in such a panic that I opened the throttle and fled past the Ace as fast as I could. Then I realised that I was being a coward so at the next intersection I

Father Bill's idea was a bold one as he intended to hold a service of dedication specially for motorcyclists in which their machines would actually be brought into church to be blessed. But first he had to publicise the event. This is one of the original handbills he distributed . . . and not without some trepidation as Father Bill explains.

Father Bill in the lion's den. The chap in the pullover standing with his back to the window is Garth Pettitt of the Sunbeam Club who later became head of the United Nations and Commonwealth Department at the Overseas Development Administration. Although a highly respected civil servant, he remained a motorcycle fanatic at heart and rode to Whitehall on one of his three bikes, changing from his leathers once he got to work. He was killed in a road accident in May 1992.

turned back. Again panic seized me and I went past. Then I turned back a second time and finally rode into the forecourt. By this time the Ace was practically deserted.

I ordered a cup of tea and sat drinking it, my face crimson with embarrassment. I left for home without getting rid of a single poster. But I consoled myself with the fact that I had at least penetrated into the lions' den, even if the lions were in fact out on the prowl.

Several weeks went by before I made my next attempt to reach the boys at the Ace. In fact it was the night before the service was due to take place that I finally summoned enough courage to go round the North Circular again. This time I made no attempt to conceal my collar and I went armed with a bundle of leaflets which said: 'This is a personal invitation to YOU to come to church next Sunday for a special service for motor-cyclists.'

It must have been about eight o'clock on the Saturday evening when once again I entered the forecourt at the Ace. It was packed with bikes. Hundreds of boys were milling around, laughing and talking.

'This is it,' I thought. 'I shall almost certainly lose my trousers or land up in the canal.'

I rode up to the nearest group and went straight to the point. 'I want you all to come to church tomorrow.'

'I was there when old Bill Shergold rolled in on a Speed Twin one day,' recalls Noddy. 'He was fully kitted up with all the leathers — brand new. Mad Bill and Blond Bob and I were sitting by the bus stop. He rode up and started talking to us and then Bill noticed that he had a dog-collar on. 'You a Reverend, are you?' asked Mad Bill. He replied that he was so Bill said: 'Well why don't you rev up and f**k off.' I said to Bill: 'Don't be like that' and the Reverend looked at me. 'Would you like a cup of tea?' he asked. 'Good idea,' and he went and bought us all teas.'

Looking back I am amazed at my own nerve — I, a middle-aged clergyman invading the stronghold of one of the toughest groups of youngsters in the country. There was no joking, no mickey taking. Instead they came crowding round, bombarding me with questions: 'What's it all about? Where is it? How do we get there?'

Someone brought me a cup of tea. I never got inside the Ace at all — people kept coming to talk with me outside. All in all it was the most fantastic evening I have ever spent. At midnight I managed to get away to snatch some sleep before making final preparations for the service at three o'clock the next day.

Rev. William Shergold, Link, 1966

Father Bill is flanked by Graham Sullivan on his left and Irish Dick (see page 48).

PRESS RELEASE ..... THE ETON COLLEGE MISSION

HACKNEY WICK, LONDON, E.9   May 7th.1962.

MOTOR CYCLES IN CHURCH.

An Ariel "Square Four", the Vicar's "Speed Twin", a mud-caked Scrambles machine, "Tina" the latest thing in Scooters , and a humble Moped - all lined up in front of the chancel screen! The occasion - a special Service of Dedication for Motor Cyclists and Scooter Riders at the Church of the Eton Mission, Eastway, Hackney Wick on Sunday May 13th. at 3 p.m. The service is being arranged by the Eton Mission and the Triumph Owners' Motor Cycle Club and has the backing of the Hackney Road Safety Committee. It will be attended by riders from a wide area of north and east London. Many will be members of organised Clubs but unattached riders are welcome and so are the Coffee Bar Cowboys. In fact we are expecting a contingent from the famous Ace Cafe on the North Circular Road.

During the course of the service Mr.Bob Matthews, the General Secretary of the Triumph Owners's Club will ask the Vicar to "bless these machines and all our machines and pray for us on our journeys..." The Vicar will then bless the machines and lead the congregation in a short act of Dedication. The purpose of this somewhat unusual service is to help the motorcyclist to see his machine not just as an exciting plaything to be used for his own selfish pleasure but as a fine piece of machinery, capable of being used to God's glory and for the benefit of other people.

SUMMARY

FRIDAY MAY 11th.
   Film Show for Motor Cyclists and Scooter Riders in the Eton Mission halls - organised by the Hackney Road Safety Committee.   8 p.m.

SUNDAY MAY 13th.
   Service of Dedication in the Church of the Eton Mission   3 p.m.

Before and after both these events the Eton Mission Coffee Bar will be open.

FOR FURTHER DETAILS PLEASE PHONE THE VICAR OF THE ETON MISSION (The Rev.W.F.Shergold)
                                   AMHerst 5475 or 5982

Father Bill outlined his objects in his press release.

The 'ton up' boys went to church yesterday — in their black leather jackets and high boots. In front of the altar, at St. Mary of Eton, Hackney Wick, stood a row of shining new motorbikes. And the boys to whom a 'ton' — 100 m.p.h. — is commonplace, heard the vicar, Father William Shergold, say in his service of thanksgiving and dedication: 'We pray Thee to bless and hallow these machines and grant that we may use them always to the glory and for the good of our fellow men.'

The 20-odd 'ton-up' boys came across London from the Ace Cafe, their headquarters on the North Circular road, for the service. Said 16-year-old Colin McCormack, of Wembley, afterwards: 'I'd come again — it makes you feel good to have been to church.'

Another teenager said: 'I don't usually go to church, but I would if it was all arranged and we could all go together.'

Father Shergold said: 'I'm going down to the Ace soon for a 'spin' on the back of one of these bikes.'

Daily Herald, May 14, 1962

Motorcycles were pushed into a church yesterday for a service of thanksgiving and dedication of motorcyclists and scooter riders. A red 500 c.c. twin cylinder machine was among them.

It belongs to the man who conducted the service — the Rev. William Shergold, vicar of St. Mary of Eton, Hackney Wick, London.

In the 60-strong congregation were young men and their girlfriends dressed in black leather. Gleaming crash helmets were at their feet.

In his sermon, Rev. Shergold said he wanted motorcyclists to be the knights-errant, of the 20th century. The majority of people thought of them as a lot of irresponsible hooligans.

'Those who criticise us have nothing constructive to offer. Let us have our wonderful machines. Let's take a pride in them, lavish our affection on them, by all means, do the ton if we want, provided that it is in the right place and at the right time. Let's use our machines, but not just for our selfish pleasure.'

'This service was not done just as a stunt, not just for publicity,' said Rev. Shergold. 'It was not done just to have a collection of interesting bikes in the courtyard.'

Western Daily Press, May 14, 1962

Eighty leather-jacketed motorcyclists took their machines to the church of St. Mary of Eton in Hackney at the invitation of the vicar, the Rev. William Shergold, himself a motorcyclist.

His own machine was one of eight lined up in front of the altar for a special service of thanksgiving and dedication.

'We bless and hallow these machines and all our machines,' said the vicar. 'May God grant that we use them always to this glory and to the good of our fellowmen.'

In a sermon based on the story of the Good Samaritan, Rev. Shergold said motorcyclists should become 'knights errant of 1962.' He added they had to face the fact that motorcyclists had got a bad name. Many people thought of them as a lot of irresponsible hooligans.

'In spite of having a dog collar when I took my first test I was unlucky to have to face a woman examiner who had a dislike for parsons and an even greater dislike for motorcyclists, so she failed me. As if to turn the knife in the wound she told me I was a menace to the country.'

New Zealand Press Report, May 15, 1962

Quatre-vingts jeunes motorcyclists, filles et garcons, en blouson de cuir noir, 'jeans' et bottes de cowboys, ont fait bénir leurs machines en l'église anglicane de Ste-Mary d'Eton, à Hackney, faubourg populeux de l'East End de Londres.

Le Soir (France), May 16, 1962

'What a wonderful response. It's amazing. I never anticipated that it would be like this.' That was what the Rev. William Shergold — the 38-year-old vicar of the Eton Mission Church — told me after Sunday's special motorcyclists' service. He was particularly surprised at the response received from the 'coffee-bar boys' of the Ace Cafe on the North Circular Road. He told me that he was a bit wary about the lads reaction, so he went down there on his Speed Twin, with a scarf over his clerical collar. But when he told them about the service, they were enthusiastic and accepted him completely. The manager of the café, in fact, rang him up this week and said that the service was the boys' sole topic of conversation for days.

Leyton Express, May 18, 1962

The response was overwhelming . . . . right round the world.

Along the M1 to Meriden yesterday came the Rev. William Shergold, the motorcycling vicar of St. Mary of Eton, Hackney Wick, London, who, hoping he might help young 'ton-up' motorcyclists to develop a greater sense of responsibility, arranged a service for them and invited them to take their machines. He pays regular visits to a café on the North Circular Road where the 'ton-up' riders meet.

He is a member of the North London branch of the Triumph Owners' Club and his purpose in the Midlands was to visit the Triumph factory. 'I am not very mechanically minded,' he explained 'and by seeing the motorcycles made, I hope to be able to talk more intelligently to the lads who ride them.'

Rev. Shergold's is a 500 c.c. model finished in red. Did he manage to get the 'ton up' on the M1?

'No,' he said. 'I did not try. I am still running my machine in — it's only a month old. I only did between 55 and 60 miles an hour.'

The Birmingham Post, May 24, 1962

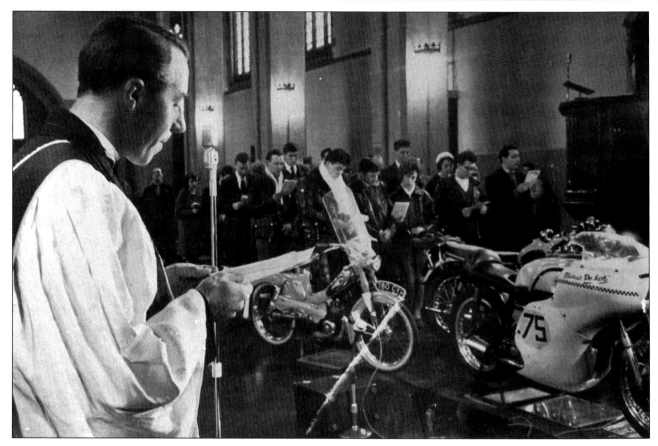

London — Dozens of teenagers took their motorcycles to church yesterday. A row of the shiny new vehicles stood in front of the altar at St. Mary of Eton, in the East End suburb of Hackney, for a service of thanksgiving and dedication. The Anglican vicar, Rev. William F. Shergold, 38, is himself a motorcyclist. One of the machines before the altar was his. The teenagers, wearing black leather jackets and black boots and carrying crash helmets, knelt while the vicar prayed that they would 'so ride that other people may be safe on the road.'

Press report,
Springfield Massachusetts, May 1962

Father Bill: 'Looking back I suppose it was a bit of a gimmick to have the bikes in church. I never intended it that way. People bring cabbages and marrows to church for the Harvest Festival and no one complains. It seemed to me perfectly natural for those who love motor bikes to bring them into God's house. I can't imagine how we got through the service at all. There were photographers and cameramen everywhere. Yet despite all these distractions there was a wonderful atmosphere of devotion and reverence.'

Everyone who read the *Daily Mirror*'s article on the motorcyclists' service must have been surprised, on looking at the accompanying photograph, to see that a 1960 Greeves Scottish in standard trim was one of the machines that had just been out and done a 'ton.'

I have ridden a current model every year since 1958 and have yet to reach this speed. The only explanation can be that, as the photo is not very good, there may be a supercharger fitted to the offside of the cylinder, or even a small rocket housed in the right-hand rear-fork member!

A. J. Maynard,
writing to The Motor Cycle, May 24, 1962

Father Bill: 'On the Tuesday several papers published cartoons, the most famous of which was by Giles in the *Daily Express* with the caption: "Last one out's chicken". I wrote and told Giles how much I had liked his picture and to my delight he sent me the original drawing signed by himself. This is one of my most treasured possessions and occupies a place of honour in my study. I was a bit overwhelmed by all this publicity. But for me it had one great advantage. I couldn't care less about having my picture in the papers. What did please me was that almost overnight I had made friends with the boys at the Ace. Press cuttings and photographs poured in to the vicarage, so I took them up to the Ace and showed them around.'

IT'S CHILDISH for a great national daily to spread anti-motor-cyclist propaganda. You generalise about "ton-up" brethren in leather jackets and poke fun at the vicar who held the service for motor-cyclists. Don't you realise that for every black sheep who behaves irresponsibly, there are thousands of decent motor-cyclists at least as good, and in many cases better, road users than the average week-end car driver?

M. H. SHORTLAND,
Boughton-lane, Moulton, Northants.

I PROTEST against Giles's cartoon, which I consider to be in extremely bad taste. It appears that motor-cyclists cannot even attend a church service without arousing adverse criticism. At a time when the motor-cycle movement is trying to recover lost prestige, the least you can do is present motor-cyclists as rational human beings and not as a set of "ton-up boys"—who form a despised minority.

P. GODWIN,
Humber-road, London, S.E.

Daily Express readers comments as published on May 22, 1962.

Having become a 'star' overnight, Keystone photographer Peter Hall went along to Eton Mission on June 29 to do a photo shoot of the vicar on a motorcycle. Reverend Shergold remembers how he had to lend him a pullover before taking him to the Ace on the pillion of his Speed Twin. But first there had to be a shot of Father Bill riding the bike in his cassock! 'The lads were delighted at receiving some good publicity for a change,' wrote Father Bill later. 'In the past any mention of them in the press had been unfavourable. I soon became a regular visitor at the Ace and got to know some of the lads quite well. One of them even invited me to his home to have lunch with his family. Others began to tell me about their mates in hospital. At this time, also, I received considerable "fan" mail, some of it complimentary, some of it not so nice. One anonymous letter warned me of the dire consequences that would follow if I continued to associate with these "leather-hearted louts".'

Cecil Richards on the left came to Britain from the West Indies in 1958 and lived local to the Ace in Village Way. When he was 16 he bought his first bike — a Tiger Cub — but exchanged it as soon as he had passed his test for a BSA Super Rocket. 'One day I was racing some of the boys up Fryent Way,' recalls Cecil, 'but when I approached the roundabout at Kingsbury, I realised I was going too fast to make the turn. So I just held on tight and carried on straight over the top. When I came out the other side I only just missed a van, but at least I came out in front of the others! On another occasion I was racing up Blackbird Hill, trying to catch the boys up thinking that I was the last one, but when I looked round there was a police motorcyclist right behind me. He stopped me but in his haste to book me his bike fell off its stand. While he went to his bike I roared off up the road and he couldn't have got my number because I never heard another word. I remember another day when I had gone up to the Busy Bee with a girl but I had to get her back by a certain time. We left there too late so, with her on the back, I was really "going to town" coming through Kingsbury when I realised we were being followed by the police. I decided I had got to lose him and so turned off down a side road only to find it was a dead end. The copper stopped at the end of the road and waited for me to come out. "What do you think you are doing," he said, "turning down here and spoiling my fun!" I explained why I was in a hurry and he let me off with a parting shot: "Well look after the young lady and for goodness sake take it easy!" Cecil still retains fond memories of the Ace: 'The first day I went down there I made the biggest mistake of all by giving a hand signal as I turned in. I was greeted by a massive welcome cheer as you never ever gave a hand signal when entering the car park!'

A Motor Cyclist's Prayer

O God,

I thank you for the marvel of a motor cycle - alive and powerful at my touch - a thing of tremendous possibilities, wonderful or terrible.

Help me to acquire the skill to control it wisely, like a tool shaping a better life for myself and those around.

I thank you for the promise of adventure each time I start; the thrill of the open road - far places - strange sights - new friends.

Make me aware as I ride around signalling, stopping, waiting, turning, zooming ahead that I am not dealing merely with THINGS - lorries, cars, bicycles, taxis - but with PEOPLE. People such as I know; people such as I am . . . making mistakes, perhaps, but not really wanting to.

Because I like people and above all because I know how precious they are to you, let me be alert, courteous, patient, considerate of the rights of others on the road, gracious enough to give up some of my own rights. And always let me be careful, realizing that another's pain would destroy my pleasure, another's loss would rob my gain, and the life I save is just as precious as my own. Amen

'Soon after the initial service which had started the club off,' explains Father Bill, 'an American motorcyclist sent me a copy of a prayer which they circulated amongst their club members. I thought it was very good indeed so I adapted it slightly and had it printed as a little card which would fit in people pockets. I wasn't quite sure how to get it around so, quite sort of daring, I wrote to the Editor of the *Daily Mirror* and asked him if he could possibly mention it. He did and the response was enormous. I don't know how many thousands we distributed. Club members also carried them around with them along with their membership cards which also had on the back: "If I am involved in an accident, please call this number" and it had the vicarage telephone number which could be called any time, day or night.' That same month the Government began their campaign for crash helmets.

A vicar is handing out copies of the Motor-Cyclists' Prayer to boys who love speed. He tours cafes in his parish on his own powerful motorcycle and asks the youngsters to use the prayer daily. The vicar is the Rev. William Shergold of St. Mary of Eton, Hackney Wick, London.

The prayer was sent to Rev. Shergold by an American motorcycle club. The vicar has had it printed in blue on small cards. He said last night: 'I want to distribute them as widely as possible especially among the coffee-bar cowboy types. 'I plan to give them out as I visit their cafes, but this is a slow business.'

Daily Mirror, July 4, 1962

The Government have decided to seek powers to compel riders on motorcycles to wear crash helmets. When the Road Traffic Bill was before the Commons standing committee Mr. Hay, Parliamentary Secretary, Ministry of Transport, promised to consider doing this after he had heard M.P.s arguing in favour of compulsion.

A new Clause, published yesterday, will be moved by Mr. Marples, Minister of Transport, when the Bill is considered on report in the Commons on Tuesday. This would enable regulations to be made requiring, subject to specified exceptions, persons "driving or riding (otherwise than in sidecars) motorcycles of any class or description" defined in the regulations to wear protective headgear.

The regulations would make different provision in relation to different circumstances. A person failing to comply would be liable on summary conviction to a fine not exceeding £50.

The standing joint committee of the R.A.C., the A.A., and the Royal Scottish Automobile Club said yesterday: 'The Ministry of Transport is well aware that the majority of motorcyclists already use safety helmets. Is it necessary to introduce compulsion for what is increasingly regarded as a routine safety precaution? If ever there was a case of taking a sledgehammer to crack a walnut this is it.'

The Times, July 13, 1962

A large gathering of doctor's attending a British Medical Association symposium on accident and casualty services here today heard Mr. H. Osmond-Clarke, a consultant surgeon, call for the abolition of the motor-cycle.

He said its complete lack of protection was responsible for the greatest number of deaths and serious injuries from accidents in the under-25 age group. It had been banned in many states in America.

The Times, July 27, 1962

A few days ago I had supper with keen motorcyclist Father William Shergold of the Eton College Mission. We discussed fully the pros and cons of the incredible amount of publicity obtained from his church service for riders and machines. It even made *Newsweek* magazine — and as far away as Germany TV stations were asking Father Shergold to be sure to let them know if he anticipated holding another service. I mentioned that if the Pope had blessed motorcycles in Rome it would have been accepted as a perfectly normal procedure. Why all the fuss here?

Noted helmet and blue jeans hanging in the vicarage cloakroom, and copies of motor-cycling journals alongside church magazines (case of the 'Tiger 100' lying down with the lamb?)

Started for teenagers in 1959, this Eton Mission's 59 Club, lying in a poor district of London, boasts a presentable percentage of motorcyclists. A few weeks back Princess Margaret and Lord Snowdon paid the club a visit which was a roaring success. The night I went about 700 teenagers were twisting to some 'go-music' played by the Comets — a great amateur group — presented in dramatic setting and lighting that would have done credit to a Radio City Music Hall show. No sanctimonious atmosphere here, with tepid tea from chipped cups — in short, a professionally run affair that obviously makes the kids feel they're having a real night out. There's one strict rule. All guys and gals that attend the dances must go to church Sunday.

It was also interesting to read of the woman examiner who failed the Rev. Shergold in his driving test, saying he was a 'menace to the public.' This, unfortunately, is the attitude of so many people to all motorcyclists.

Dick Wyler, Motorcyclist (USA),
August 1962

Youths and girls of 17 and 18 are nearly 10 times as likely to be injured on the roads as people of 39 or 51, according to a detailed survey. In a road safety bulletin, circulated today, a police force says: 'The motorcycle is the main factor in the astronomical rise in the accident rate to teenagers.'

About 60 per cent of the young victims receive their injuries when travelling on motorcycles, mopeds or motor-scooters, and all the teenagers killed in the country during the first half of this year were riding these machines.

Figures for the first half of this year show that 97 people aged 17 were injured, 92 aged 18, 77 aged 16, and 68 aged 19. This compares with only 10 aged 39, 11 aged 51 and 10 aged 11. The police ask 'what happens on their sixteenth birthday that suddenly makes them so accident-prone?'

The reason why teenagers are so vulnerable on a motorcycle has also been analysed by the police. Out of 156 accidents in which teenagers were to blame 40 were caused by excessive speed, 20 by overtaking improperly, 17 by inexperience, 19 by lost control and 12 by inattention.

The Times, September 25, 1962

It is difficult to imagine a more tendentious piece of figure juggling than that reported as from a survey by the Derby police in your issue of September 25 under the head 'More Killed on Motor Cycles'.

In fact, the casualty figures just issued by the M.o.T. for the period January–July show a decrease in fatalities of 226 for the moped, scooter and motorcycle group as against the same period in 1961, and as against a rise of 67 for cars, etc., while the total casualty rate in the three two-wheeler classes also fell by 10.4, 1.1, and 14.5 per cent respectively over the same period. So much for that 'astronomical rise in accident rate' quoted.

As for the age groupings, surely it must be obvious that there are 10 times as many riders aged 17 or 18 as aged 51, and just who are the 10 riders aged 11 quoted in the comparative figures?

Most drivers do their learning and gain experience on two-wheelers, becoming better drivers and more tolerant citizens because of it. Any accident rate is too high but the realities give no cause for anti-motor-cycling propaganda by the police.

Power and Pedal with the Scooter,
October 4, 1962

Within weeks his efforts were acknowledged in all quarters. Alf Hagon (who was to go on to achieve the world record for 1 kilometre standing start at 116.903 m.p.h. in October 1966) and the Superintendent of the Met Traffic Police attended the presentation of a chalice to Father Bill on January 12, 1963 'from motorcyclists the world over.'

From many letters, but above all from conversations with the boys themselves, I soon began to realise that they were virtually an outcast section of the community. Because of their dress, their noisy bikes and their tendency to move around in gangs, nobody wanted them.

Dance halls refused them, bowling alleys told them to go home and change into ordinary clothes. Youth clubs were afraid of them. Even the transport cafes didn't really welcome their custom. After all, a motorcyclist consumes on average a cup of tea or a Coke every two hours. A lorry driver or a coach tripper will spend five bob on a meal and be on his way within 30 minutes.

I was becoming more and more convinced that what they really needed was a new kind of club which would combine the personal and friendly touch of a youth club with the free and easy atmosphere of a transport cafe or coffee bar.

My difficulty was that our premises at the Eton Mission were already being used almost to capacity but eventually we decided to make use of Saturday nights — the only time when the halls were not being used — and to launch the new club in October 1962.

The question of finding a suitable personality of the motorcycling world to open the club was solved during one of my weekly visits to the Ace. I was sitting at a table drinking tea and showing photographs to a crowd of the lads when I noticed at the next table a gentleman of more than ample proportions. He introduced himself as 'Harold Harvey' and asked if he might see the photographs. It appeared that he was a photographer and often went to motorcycle race meetings to take action pictures. He said that he might be able to find us a suitable guest.

As a result of this chance meeting we not only secured the services of Alf Hagon on the opening night but the club acquired its first adult helper.

In order to publicise our opening night as widely as possible we prepared some handbills which I took around to places like the Busy Bee, the Dug-Out, Woodlands, Johnsons and, of course, the Ace.

As a matter of fact it was never intended that it should be a club at all — as witness the affectionate title of the Vicar's Caff which it was soon given.

Rev. William Shergold, Link, 1966

The motorcycling vicar, the Rev. Bill Shergold of Eton College Mission, Hackney Wick, London, had a motorcycling day to remember last Saturday. He married two motorcyclists from the Ace Cafe at Fulham, dashed to Paddington to marry two motorcyclists who go to his own 59 Club, and then returned to the Eton Mission to find himself on the receiving end for a change.

There, midway through the 59 Club's dance, a presentation of a solid gold and silver chalice, inscribed 'from motorcyclists the world over', was made to the Reverend Bill, as he is known to his fellow motorcyclists. The chalice, hand-made in Italy, was subscribed to by members of the 59 Club both in this country and abroad, and the presentation was made by Superintendent S. Hebbes, Traffic and Transport Officer of No. 3 District of the Metropolitan Police, acting for the Commissioner of Police.

Among those who spoke were world record holder George Brown, speedway and grass-track star Alf Hagon, Harry Louis, editor of *Motor Cycle*, and Brian McLoughlin, editor of *Motor Cycle News*.

Motor Cycle News, January 16, 1963

'One very pleasant duty in January 1963,' writes Father Bill,' was to marry Steve Hammond (see page 87), an Ace Cafe regular who was now a member of the club, to Jacqueline Mogey at Emmanuel Church, Paddington. The press pictured me in my motorcycle attire as I was off to conduct another wedding service. . . .

On his way back to work after lunch on Tuesday, a 20-year-old Hemel Hempstead motorcyclist was in collision with a lorry in St. Albans Road and died a few hours later at West Herts Hospital. He was Roger Philip Davis, of 47 Fairway. An apprentice engineer at Rotax, Maylands Avenue, he had lived in Hemel Hempstead for the past three years. Born at Berkhamsted and educated at Ashlyns School, he was a member of the famous '59 Club', in Hackney, better known as the 'Ton-Up Vicar's Club.'

Hemel Hempstead Gazette, April 26, 1963

. . . but a very unhappy side of my job was to officiate at the funerals of club members. One of the first to be killed was Roger Davis. In all, six of my boys died that first year.'

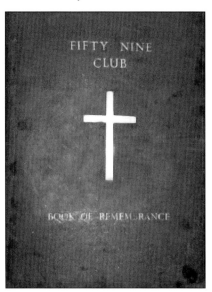

'We managed to get a nicely-bound Book of Remembrance produced so that the names of those members of the club who were killed could be entered in it. The book was divided up into months according to the date of death. When I moved to St. Mary's Paddington in May 1964 I took the club — and the book — with me although we continued to meet at Hackney until the new vicar arrived in September. The members then used to meet in my vicarage at No. 6 Park Place Villas, which was quite large, in Little Venice. The boys and girls were always in and out of it so I set up a little chapel there called The Chapel of the Way where I kept the Book of Remembrance on the altar table. Occasionally we would have a service for anyone who would like to come to remember some friend who had lost their life on the road. The book and the cross and candlesticks were dedicated to the memory of Clive Burrell — 'Buzz' — who was killed on June 2, 1964.'

1963

Gerald Bardett-Coutts
Michael Carroll
Roger Davis
Peter Manning
Christopher Lucy
John Sweeting

1964

Dennis Anderson
Clive 'Buzz' Burrell
Geoffrey Clark
Brian Evans
Brian Finch
Leslie Gedge
Allan Huggett
Michael Jefferson
Brian Morris
Gillian Ward
Norman Watts
Keith Young

1965

David Abraham
Anthony Bond
Graham Gore
David Henderson
Rodney Lee
Robert Nelson
Susan Redman
Michael Stratford
Michael Voller

1966

George Burksfield
Gordon Black
Michael Cahalin
Paul Rolfe
Peter Rose
Stephen Saunders
James Scott
Brian Weatherall

At the funeral on Wednesday of 17-year-old Michael Carroll, of Spencer Road, who died after an accident on his motorcycle, teenagers from coffee bars and youth clubs in the town attended to pay their last respects. The funeral was at Eastbourne Crematorium.

The well-known 'ton-up' vicar, the Rev. Bill Shergold, who runs a 1,000-strong youth motorcycling club at Hackney, rode his motorcycle down and attended the service dressed in black motorcycling leathers.

On Wednesday all the teenage friends of the boy arrived in vans and cars. None travelled by motorcycle.

The accident in which Michael was killed occurred on August Bank Holiday weekend in Purley Way, Croydon.

Eastbourne Chronicle, August 24, 1963

Michael Carroll, aged 17, was killed on the August Bank Holiday weekend in Purley Way, Croydon, and cremated at Eastbourne. 'Michael was on his way to the club for the first time when this terrible accident happened,' says Father Bill. 'I felt it was my duty to attend the service.'

1968

Keith Cole
Sheila Dealey
Robert Duke
John Lancaster
Barry Masters
Nigel Mileham
George McAuley
Stuart Russell
Stephen Worboys

1970

John West

1976

Michael Ian Halliday

1982

Garry George Goddard

1985

Martin Lloyd
Mark Molineux

1987

John Peppitt
Jeremy 'Jez' Taylor

1991

Keith 'Tiger Ted' Warren

UNDATED

Terence Bowen
Robert Brittain
Leslie Lavall
Barry Masters
David Reynolds
Stuart Russell
Kerry Shipton
David Twait

Ton-up boys and their girlfriends rushed to the assistance of motorcyclists involved in a crash near the Ace Cafe, North Circular Road, Stonebridge, on Saturday night. A woman died in the accident. She was Mrs. Kathleen Keane, aged 34, of 32 Clifton Avenue, Wembley, and she was riding on the pillion of a motorcycle driven by her husband, Mr. John Keane, of the same address. Mrs. Keane was thrown heavily and is believed to have somersaulted through the air before crashing on to her head. She died from head injuries. Her husband sustained a fractured collar bone and other injuries and was treated at the Central Middlesex Hospital.

Rider of the other machine involved was 18-year-old Mr. Edward William Murch, of 8 Holloway Street, Hounslow. His pillion passenger, Miss Ann Parker, aged 16, of 51 Rosecroft Gardens, Twickenham was slightly hurt.

Willesden Chronicle, March 22, 1963

'In the early days,' explains Father Bill, 'no records of attendance were kept so it is impossible to say how long it was before the membership began to grow by leaps and bounds. My impression is that it grew quite slowly at first. There was very little organisation — no subscriptions were charged, rules were kept to a minimum, and we didn't even keep a list of names and addresses. Members started wearing the small metal lapel badges which were already popular among members of the original 59 Club. The black-and-white pennants which were intended for scooterists were bought by motorcyclists and cut up to form attractive arm badges. This is how the now-famous '59' cloth arm badge came into being.'

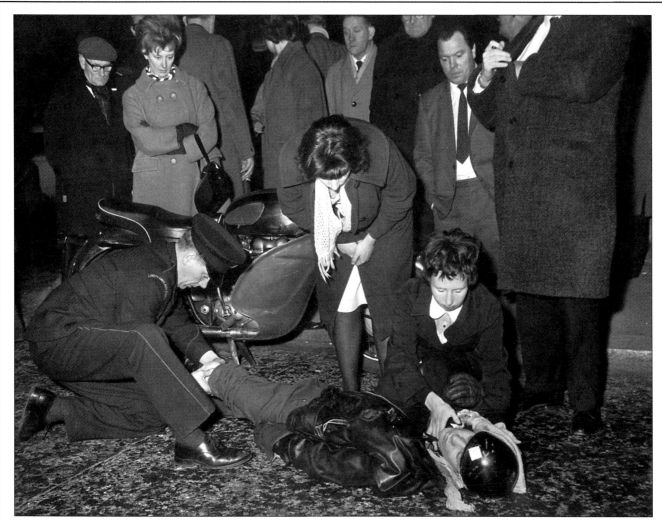

A campaign to persuade motorcyclists to wear crash helmets was announced by the Minister of Transport yesterday.

Posters and leaflets are being distributed and a circular giving 'factors likely to influence the sale of safety helmets' is being sent to motorcycle and scooter dealers. Mr. Marples said that if after six months the campaign had proved unsuccessful he would consider using his powers under the Road Traffic Act to make safety helmets compulsory.

Last year, he said, it was estimated that about 65 per cent of male riders and about 75 per cent of female riders wore safety helmets. This was only a little better than 1960 and 'a hard core of non-wearers' still remained to be convinced.

Studies by the Road Research Laboratory had disclosed that wearing a safety helmet reduced the risk of head injuries by between 30 and 40 per cent. Last year 1,255 riders and passengers on motorcycles and scooters were killed and 22,878 seriously injured; head injuries accounted for about three-quarters of the deaths.

The Times, May 28, 1963

As far back as 1946-47 when this picture was taken of the roundabout at Neasden, it had a reputation as an accident black spot. The roundabout was eliminated in 1973 when the underpass to Wembley was completed.

When asked how his new 50 m.p.h. speed limit was to be enforced, Mr. Marples airily replied 'Oh, the Police will do that.' It is going to be a considerable undertaking. A few hundred police patrol cars are somehow expected both to enforce the 50 m.p.h. limit on 750 miles of selected trunk roads at week-ends during the greater part of the summer and to enforce a 50 m.p.h. limit on all roads throughout England and Wales (other than motorways and roads with a permanent speed limit) during the five week-ends of the peak holiday period.

The Police Review, May 31, 1963

There were 516 deaths from road accidents in May, an increase of 40, or 8 per cent over May last year, the Ministry of Transport announced yesterday. Seriously injured numbered 7,306, an increase of 6 per cent, and 21,416 were slightly injured, an increase of 2 per cent.

Total casualties numbered 29,238, 3 per cent more than a year ago. There was an estimated 10 per cent increase in motor traffic. The increase in deaths occurred mainly among motorcycle riders — 72 this May, compared with 50 last year — and adult pedestrians — 144 against 117.

Total casualties among riders and passengers of motorcycles, scooters, and mopeds increased by 305 (4 per cent), and fatal and serious casualties by 203 (9 per cent), although the mileage travelled was 5 per cent less.

The Times, August 2, 1963

Short of standing in the middle of the fast lane, this is the nearest one dare reach out over the crash barrier to take a comparison. And at the Iron Bridge *(opposite)* photography is even more dangerous as the pavement which existed in the 1960s has been removed to provide an extra lane. Even so, we ventured into no-mans-land to take the comparison armed with nothing more than a yellow jacket!

Confirmation of the deadly danger of the quarter-mile bend in the North Circular Road as it passes from the Book Centre over the Iron Bridge at Neasden came this week in unmistakable fashion — three accidents within hours on Friday night, followed by a fatality on Monday.

The steadily rising accident rate on this stretch of road is bringing it a reputation as one of Willesden's worst black spots, and on Tuesday a senior police officer confirmed official anxiety about the bend and commented, 'We believe that speed is the main trouble here.'

It was about 9.50 p.m. on Friday that the first accident took place. A Ford Cortina car driven by Mr. Jack Ryding, Cambridge Road, N17 skidded near Dog Lane on the approach to the bridge and spun around.

An hour and a half later, a little further along the road, came accident number two in which five people were badly hurt. A Ford car driven by Mr. Timothy Harris, Vincent Gardens, Neasden, is reported to have mounted the centre verge, crossing into the other traffic lane, and to have collided with a Vauxhall car travelling in the opposite direction.

Five minutes after this accident came crash number three at the other end of the curve not far from the Book Centre. A Ford van skidded and crashed into a lamp post.

The man who died near the Iron Bridge on Monday was Mr. William Edward Perkins, Howard Drive, Borehamwood, Herts. He was riding a moped and is believed to have been struck by a passing van.

At the same time, a cyclist, Mr. Colin Copsey, Richmond Road, East Finchley, was struck — presumably by the same van — and thrown off his machine. Police are working on the assumption that both men were struck a glancing blow by a van as it passed by but so far its identity has not been traced.

Willesden Chronicle, November 8, 1963

One of the bridge's most well-known casualties was Alan Stacey, the Wembley Town footballer, killed in a motorcycle accident on September 15, 1959.

In January 1964, *The Leather Boys*, a film with a strong motorcycle element, was released starring Rita Tushingham, a newcomer Colin Campbell, and Dudley Sutton. The Ace features prominently and a number of the cafe regulars worked on the film as extras. Even though he was only a youngster at the time, the film had a great influence on Mark Metcalfe although he could never remember the title until it came out on video. Since then he says he must have watched the film at least 50 times and for the last ten years has searched for the locations where it was made. Mark's current bike, a Harris Matchless G80, was currently undergoing conversion to a cafe racer . . .

You have not seen her ugly-fascinating face on the cinema screen since 1961 when, as an unknown, she gave a prize-winning performance in *A Taste of Honey*.

You have not had a chance to see her second film *The Leather Boys* before, because it has been held up for nearly a year in the escape tunnel where so many independently made films have to wait for a release date.

Now, with its topicality browning slightly at the edges, this British film, produced by Raymond Stross, has finally made it through British Lion into the Empire, Leicester Square *(Cert X)* and with a release on the ABC circuit.

And Miss Rita Tushingham is with us once again to prove that beauty is about the last piece of ammunition a good actress needs.

The Leather Boys are a leather-jacketed, ton-up mob who choose as headquarters a caff conveniently close to an arterial road, and tear about on motorbikes to clear their helmeted heads of frustrations.

. . . . so when he took us on a tour of the film locations, he was bikeless . . . . but to get in the right mood he donned his 1960s jacket adorned with his film counterpart's nickname 'Dodgy'.

First stop Wimbledon Art College in Merton Hall Road ([1] on the map *opposite)* where Reggie (Colin Campbell) picks up his fiancée Dot (Rita Tushingham) from school.

Miss Tushingham is a pert little exhaust-follower, who falls straight from the arms of school into marriage with one of the boys (Reggie).

With almost painfully accurate attention to detail that shifts it straight out of the slow lane, the film looks first at a teenage marriage, and then moves on to an ever trickier relationship.

Dot, it seems, didn't get married to cook.

And Reggie, hardworking, decent, utterly bewildered, seeks solace more and more in the caff and his leathery friends.

But when he strikes up a close friendship with Pete, the trap of tragedy is set. For wise-cracking Pete, a tall blond nut of an ex-merchant seaman, is unknown to Reggie, a homosexual. Dudley Sutton, another relatively unknown in films, handles this role with quite brilliant subtlety. He etches in the

character with almost misleading ease, rightly making him both sympathetic and tragic.

It is not until the end that Reggie, in a dockside pub, sensed the truth about Pete and walks away without a word.

An intelligent film, intelligently made and beautifully acted. One will never understand why it was held up for so long.

Daily Herald, January 22, 1964

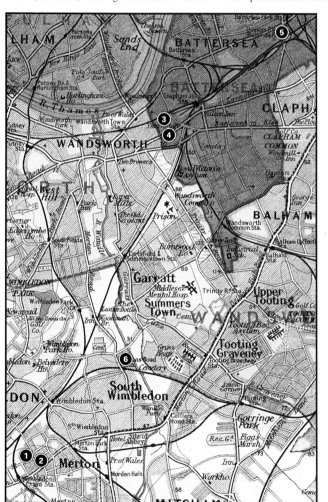

Having lived all his life in south London, and worked as a postman and later as a bus driver (on a genuine 1960s Routemaster!), Mark is very familiar with the area which helped him enormonously in his search. Another link was that his mum had worked at the Merton Park Studios [2], since demolished on Kingston Road, which made the film.

It took ages for Mark to discover the street used for Reggie's home. Initially, Mark was misled into thinking that the large industrial complex vaguely visible at the end of the road was Battersea Power Station but none of the streets seemed to match. Then he remembered that in the 1960s there used to be another power station across the river at Fulham and, by drawing sight lines on a map of the roads that lined up with it, thought it might be Harbut Road [3] in Wandsworth. Well it certainly looks possible . . .

. . . and it is! Well done Dodgy! No. 3 still stands at the end of the road.

And just round the corner in St. John's Hill, Mark found the flat [4] where Reggie and Dot live after they are married.

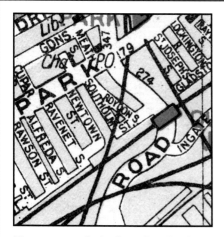

The quest to find where Dot lived was only solved when a mate of Mark's, 'Boot Fair Bob' bought an old ambulance map of London as it was in the 1960s. After a long search, he found a spot where the unusual street layout of two railway arches and a protruding building matched — at Southolm Street [5] near Battersea Park.

'You'd never find an Ace boy wearin' them jeans,' the girl said disparagingly. It was two in the morning and we stood with the mobile generators and the lines of motorbikes in the forecourt of the Ace Cafe on the North Circular Road. The arc lights caught the fine rain looking like threads of cotton, slanting down into the puddles on the tarmac. In the shadows were about 150 of the Ace regulars, many of them now working as extras. In the foreground were the actors, and the considerable number of people who form a film unit.

The message reached Sidney Furie, the young Canadian who was directing *The Leather Boys*.

'One of the kids says Colin would never go on a burn-up in those jeans.'

'Okay, we'll change them. Thanks.'

'E'd wear leather. And big white socks turned down over 'is boots,' added the girl.

When the jeans were brought the following night they were plastic, but you can't tell the difference on the screen, they say. Under the strip lighting of the Ace they looked just a little shinier than the black leather everyone else was wearing. But the initial nerves on both sides soon subsided.

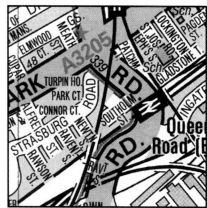

But when Mark reached the spot he found that Roydon Street (from where Reggie is seen emerging in the film) had been expunged from the map. Strasburg Road has since been cut through the site and a block of flats built on the site of the house.

Mark had already recognised the church used for Dot and Reggie's wedding in Kohat Road [6] in South Wimbledon.

The 49 bus with Clapham Junction on its indicator board, used to take the wedding party to the reception, is a red herring

because this is a side road, not a bus route. One can even see in this still how the bus stop has been set in the pavement.

'Rita's marvellous,' said one boy. 'I 'ad toothache and she went round everyone findin' me an aspirin.' This was George, Colin Campbell's stand-in who contributed some of the most daring and exciting riding in the film. He and Ron — who rode for Dudley Sutton, the other lead — were responsible for the maintenance of the bikes and were infinitely patient. I'm not sure if they were among those who lost their jobs because of the five weeks absence they took. Those who did didn't care.

At the end of the Kohat Road, the bus, followed by the gang of motorcyclists (from the Ace), turns left down Haydons Road

en route to the wedding reception (which was filmed in the King's Head in Merton High Street).

Left: **One of the most remarkable discoveries — supposedly somewhere en route to Scotland — was found by Mark at the** Devil's Punchbowl on the A3 in Hampshire! *Right:* **Mark with Fiona and his beloved Beagle Zack on the same bench.**

Many made a point of taking me to one side and assuring me that the ton-ups weren't as black as they thought I'd painted them.

'I don't beat no one up, like that gang at Finchley. We do the ton sometimes, but not where any one's goin' to get 'urt. If we come off, it's our own look-out, ain't it?'

Among the more responsible element was Dosser, who told me 'I want to get some of them off the road, next year, and on to the race track'. He didn't elaborate.

'Are you all here, every night?'

'Except Saturdays. We go down the Vicar's then. 'E wears leather, jus' like us.'

There was general disappointment on the evening the police caught one of the boys speeding.

'E's stupid to do it tonight, with all this goin' on. What 'e want to go an' do it tonight for?' They felt they had been let down.

Grace, [*another pseudonym for Jenny Wittich — see page 175 Ed*] Ron's girlfriend [*she was now his wife — Ed*], was one of the two girls who eventually went to Scotland. She was tall and beautiful, with long brown hair and high cheekbones, and wore boys' black leather jeans.

'Did you enjoy it?' I asked her when she returned.

'It made a change,' she said. 'The Lake District was lovely.'

'The hotel in Edinburgh was really posh,' added Rita's stand-in. It is surprising how on the bikes the difference between stand-in and star is undetectable. 'It was like a holiday.'

The final scene on the North Circular was shot on a cold Friday morning, the director and the cameraman both wearing the tartan woolly berets they had bought in Scotland. The Ace was full of lorry drivers, only a few of the boys and girls who fill the place at night.

New Statesman, February 21, 1964

The final location, discovered by Nigel Stark. Dodgy walks away from the Tidal Basin Tavern which still stands at the western end of the Royal Victoria Dock in east London. (For more scenes shot at the Ace itself, see pages 143, 161, 168 and 169.)

Although *The Leather Boys* had been made in the autumn of 1962, it was not released to the cinemas — with an over 18 'X' certificate — until January 1964. The New Year was a watershed in many ways. Mary Quant set the ball rolling when she opened her new Chelsea boutique on the 13th, with emphasis on the mini-skirt. February saw American teenagers give an ecstatic reception to the Beatles, who were already riding high in Britain with having had four Top-Ten hits, and in March Radio Caroline began broadcasting from a ship anchored outside Britain's territorial waters in the North Sea and within six months had more listeners than the BBC. Revolution by the young — the 'wild ones' as the press labelled them — against the old order had began and Clacton on the Essex coast became the first battleground. During the Easter weekend at the end of March, leatherclad motorcycling 'Rockers' clashed with the new breed of smartly-dressed, scooterborne 'Mods' who had chosen the town for their Bank Holiday excursion.

A gang of teenage motorcycle hoodlums came from a church youth club, police said yesterday. A vicar who rides a powerful motorcycle founded the club to turn out well-behaved 'ton-up' boys.

Police at Margate, Kent, said the majority of the troublemakers who started a pitched battle in the town on Easter Monday, were from the 59 Club, Hackney Wick in East London. At one time, 85 of them were counted outside the Dreamland amusement park where a youth was stabbed after a fight between 'Mods' and 'Rockers'.

Senior officers of Kent police are to consider setting up a mobile 'flying squad' to rush to seaside towns when trouble starts. One officer said, 'Margate had just eight men and four special constables on duty to deal with a rioting mob of over 100 ton-up boys on Monday night.'

In Clacton, Essex, an emergency meeting of the resort's hotel and guest house association is to be called to discuss damage 'done' to the town's business by the Easter riots by teenage toughs. Hotels reported that holidaymakers have been scared away and have begun cancelling bookings.

Daily Mail, April 1, 1964

Daily Mirror

After Clacton .. a new battlefield

WILD ONES 'BEAT UP' MARGATE

3d. Monday, May 18, 1964 ★ ★ ★ No. 18,788

30 arrested in all-day clashes

By MIRROR REPORTER

THE wild ones—self-styled Mods and Rockers—picked the Kent resort of Margate to beat up for Whitsun. All day yesterday the rival teenagers fought and smashed their way around the town.

When it got dark, about 800 Mods were parading around Margate. Two hundred Rockers were lurking in a quiet corner of the town.

At least thirty youths had been arrested. And there was blood on the sands.

Most of the Mods had arrived on scooters bristling with headlights and badges. Most of the leather-jacketed Rockers had roared into town on shiny motor-cycles.

Wrecking

Many of the teenagers turned up late on Saturday night. They got down to the wrecking and smashing right away.

At 10.30 yesterday morning, the big battle broke out—as 500 Mods attacked 100 Rockers.

Six policemen stepped in, truncheons waving — and both mobs turned on them. Soon after that raging Mods swarmed through Margate's High-street, smashing windows.

All afternoon, the rival gangs fought small skirmishes.

Extra police poured into the town from as far as fifty miles away.

But, at Kent's county police headquarters, at Maidstone, a spokesman said: "The situation at Margate is in hand."

Clashed

At Clacton, Essex—beaten up by 1,000 teenagers at Easter—no trouble was reported yesterday.

At Skegness, Lincs, about fifty youths clashed with staff of a cafe on Saturday night. Four youths will appear in court.

At Devil's Dyke, a Sussex beauty spot near Brighton, twenty Mods beat up a cafe early yesterday.

Later, ten boys were arrested in Brighton and charged with stealing food.

Girls who followed the wild ones—Page 3
The Battle of Margate Sands —Centre Pages

HEAD WELL DOWN . . An arrested youth is carried off, head down, by policemen at Margate. The constable on the left has a black eye. And the sergeant has lost his helmet in the scuffle.

HANDS FULL One policeman, truncheon out, struggles to hold two youths at once on Margate sands.

Further clashes followed during the summer, press reporting being blamed for exacerbating the problem leading to copycat disturbances' at Margate, Hastings and Brighton.

The Brighton fracas was later the subject of another film, this time with an enigmatic title: *Quadrophenia*. Although made 15 years after the event, nevertheless it captured the imagery of the time as the cavalry rode in to do battle!

With unfavourable reports in the press ringing in his ears that some of his 59-ers had been involved, that same month Reverend Shergold was in the middle of the move to Paddington Green. *Right:* **His new church lay on the north side of Harrow Road.** *Below:* **This entrance, emerging into fast traffic, was later closed off and landscaped.**

Hundreds of motorcyclists and their girl-friends, in black leather jackets and crash helmets, converged on Paddington Green on Friday evening. They had come to watch the institution and induction of the 'ton-up' vicar,' the Rev. W. F. Shergold, as Vicar of St. Mary's, Paddington.

More than 200 of them crowded into the tiny church with the Mayor and Mayoress of Paddington, Councillor. Major James Collins and Mrs. Collins, Police Superintendent. A. Selway, members of the council and the regular congregation. They filled every seat and stood at the back and on the stairs leading up to the gallery. More than a hundred, unable to get in, waited outside to cheer Rev. Shergold when he emerged.

Police from Paddington Green station were on special duty to control the traffic and direct the motorcyclists to park their machines on the recreation ground behind the church. After the ceremony a huge crowd poured into Paddington Town Hall, where a reception had been arranged by the church council.

A member of the council staff, directing a queue of motorcyclists into the council chamber when the vestibule was already full, gasped: 'I have no idea how many are here — it's impossible to estimate.'

All the motorcyclists belong to the club which Rev. Shergold started for them as an off-shoot of his church youth club in Hackney. Now it is being transferred to Paddington.

Kilburn Times, May 8, 1964

But there was good news to counter the bad as Father Bill explains: 'The vicar at St. Martin's-in-the-Fields invited the club to take part in the distribution and collection of envelopes for Christian Aid. So a huge mob of us arrived in Trafalgar Square *(opposite)* **and were blessed by the vicar who gave out packs of publicity material and envelopes for distributing to the churches in London.'**

It was an unbelievable sight and sound. The forecourt of St. Martin-in-the-Fields, Trafalgar Square, echoed to the roar of nearly 100 powerful motorcycles ridden by Rockers and their girlfriends.

A crowd watched puzzled. 'What are those Rockers up to now?' asked a woman. One of the ton-up boys gave the answer. 'We're doing something good and worthwhile,' he said. And so they were. The Rockers gave up yesterday afternoon to help launch a campaign in aid of starving people overseas.

By their mercy mission, the 59 Club boys were hoping to restore something of the Rockers' prestige after the outrages of Margate and Clacton. Ronald Colman, 21, of Battersea, said: 'We feel fed up with what happened in the seaside towns — Rockers who do that sort of thing are just ignorant, and we feel thoroughly ashamed of them.'

Chris Robins, a 19-year-old clerk, from Belvedere, Kent, said: 'I know that a lot of people would not believe us, but we enjoy doing something to help others in need. 'The lot of us who wear black leathers and ride bikes have been classed as wild ones. But we don't go looking for trouble and we don't smash people's property.'

Final word from the leather-clad ton-up vicar, Mr. Shergold: 'I believe these Rockers are all fundamentally decent youngsters.

It's just that you have to give them love, in other words, understanding. Give the Rockers a lead and they will do things like fixing up old people's homes, laying lino and even providing old people with TV sets. That's what my lads have done.'

Sunday Mirror, May 24, 1964

'The vicar was very impressed with the way the boys behaved and the publicity it got him.' *Above:* **St Martin's . . . 1964 . . . 2002!**

Casualties to motorcyclists and their passengers increased by 92.2 per cent in February compared with the corresponding month last year, the Royal Society for the Prevention of Accidents states in its statistical review, published yesterday.

Casualties to riders of motor-scooters and their passengers rose by 84.7 per cent and to moped riders by 71.8 per cent.

February's casualties totalled 24,526 including 551 deaths, compared with 20,610 and 356 dead the previous year.

On a mile-for-mile basis, the accident rate for motorcycles and scooters was about five times that for motor cars: motor scooter, 50,000: motorcycle 52,250; moped, 102,500.

The Times, May 12, 1964

TERRY — BOY OF MY DREAMS

Terry! Terry!

He said to me, he wanted to be, near to me.
He said he never, wanted to be, out of my sight.
But it's too late to get this boy my love tonight.
Please wait at the gate of Heaven for me, Terry.

He said to me, he wanted to be, close by my side.
We had a quarrel, I was untrue, on the night he died.
And it's too late to tell this boy how great he was.
Please wait at the gate of Heaven for me, Terry.

He rode into the night,
Accelerated his motor bike.
I cried to him in fright,
Don't do it! Don't do it! Don't do it!

He said to me, you are the one, I want to be with.
He said to me, you are the one whom my love I shall give.
One day he'll know how hard I prayed for him to live.
Please wait at the gate of Heaven for me, Terry.

WORDS AND MUSIC © LYNN RIPLEY

Jennifer Jenkins was a nurse at Wembley Hospital: 'My memories of the Ace Cafe are of nursing the boys with fractured femurs and head injuries following accidents. Sadly their injuries were so severe that some died. My first experience with death was when I specialised a lad of 18 or 19 for a week on night duty. When he died — on my day off — I felt as if I had lost a dear friend, even if we never spoke as he had been in a coma all that time.'

With a hugh increase reported in the two-wheeler death toll, 17-year-old Lynn Ripley recorded her biker anthem *Terry*. Twinkle's song entered the charts in November 1964 and stayed there for 20 weeks, reaching No. 4 in the hit parade.

REQUIEM FOR A ROCKER

Leather-Jacket boys ride up to bid a friend farewell

By MICHAEL WARD

HALF-A-DOZEN "ton-up boys" did a steady five miles an hour in London yesterday out of respect to one of their friends who died after a motorcycle accident.

They joined Father Bill Shergold, the motorcycling priest who founded their "59 club," at the funeral of Michael Sheehan, 29-year-old storekeeper.

He died in hospital from head injuries six days after his motorcycle combination crashed into a stationary van in Minerva-road, Park Royal.

WIFE WATCHED

His wife, Julie, mother of a 17-month-old baby, watched outside her home in Kilburn Park-road, Kilburn, as the ton-up boys and girls quietly drove up on their machines.

Wearing their leather jackets and reinforced riding boots, they handed in wreaths shaped as wheels and another as an Isle of Man trophy.

NOT SPEEDING

Father Shergold, dressed like the club members, said: "Michael was one of my first members in the 59 Club. He was an expert cyclist and fully competent.

"None of us knows exactly what happened."

The 'Leather Boys' turned out in force to say goodbye to their friend, 29-year-old Michael Sheehan of Kilburn Park Road, Kilburn on Wednesday morning. Michael Sheehan, who had raced at the Snetterton and Brands Hatch circuits, died in Wembley Hospital on Friday following a motorcycling accident a week ago. He leaves a 21-year-old widow and a baby of 17 months. Twenty-five 'ton-up' boys 'escorted' the funeral cortege to Kensal Green cemetery. They stood at the graveside with relatives and other friends of Michael. Also with the mourners at Kensal Green was the Rev. W. F. Shergold of St. Mary's Church, Paddington Green.

Willesden Chronicle, November 27, 1964

The very same week that Twinkle was in the charts, Father Bill attended the funeral of Michael Sheehan who had been one of the first members of the club (although for some reason his name does not appear in the Book of Remembrance — see page 119). His overgrown grave lies in Plot 179 in Kensal Green Cemetery, Harrow Road.

A month later the US female vocal group, the Shangri-Las, entered the British chart with *Leader of the Pack*. Both records were in the hit parade at the same time although the Shangri-Las only reached No. 11. The group were two sets of sisters — Betty and Mary Weiss and Marge and Mary Ann Ganser — from Jackson High School in Queens although for some reason it is rare to see all four girls pictured together. The song which propelled them into stardom was written by an aspiring record producer, George Morton, and released in the States by Red Bird. The record came out again in the UK seven years later when it rose to No. 3 and it had a third revival in 1976 when it reached the No. 7 position.

LEADER OF THE PACK

'Is she really going out with him?'
'Well there she is, let's ask her.'
'Betty, is that Jimmy's ring you're wearing?'
'Mmm, hmmm.'
'Gee, it must be great riding with him. Is he
    picking you up after school today?'
'Nnn Mmm.'
'By the way, where'd you meet him?'
'I met him at the candy store. Turned around
    and smiled at me — you get the picture?'
'Yes we see it.'
'That's when I fell for the Leader of the Pack.'

My folks were always putting him down
They said he came from the wrong side of town
They told me he was bad
But I know he was sad
That's why I fell for the Leader of the Pack.
One day my dad said find someone new.
I had to tell my Jim we were through
He stood there and asked me why
All I could do was cry
I'm sorry, I hurt you, Leader of the Pack.

'I saw his smile and as I kissed him goodbye
the tears were beginning to show. As he drove
away, on that rainy night, I begged him to
go slow. Whether he heard, I'll never know
Look out! Look out! Look out!'

I felt so helpless what could I do
Remembering all the things we'd been through
And so they all stop and said
I can't hide my tears but I don't care
I'll never forget him, the Leader of the Pack.

The Leader of the Pack . . . Now he's gone . . .

Father Bill Shergold, the motorcycling priest who founded the famed '59 Club,' seeks a new international headquarters for his 7,000 young members. It will be the biggest of its kind in the world, with every possible sporting sideline that Father Bill can find cash for.

Daily Express, November 19, 1964

Meanwhile Father Bill continued his mission to support his young motorcyclists. 'At first the boys would meet in the vicarage but in April 1965 we opened formal premises in the hall across the road in Unwin Place. The following month we launched our magazine *Link*. These lads are reading the first issue in my sitting room.'

'After our successful day at St. Martin's I realised that I needed a curate to help with the day-to-day running of the show. I knew a young curate in East London in West Hackney who rode a bike – his name was Graham Hullett *(far left)* — and, with a grant from the Inner London Education Authority, he came to help with the club in April 1967. He was in fact a trained teacher which qualified him for the grant as a club leader. When I left Paddington to go to Dover, he took over as full-time leader of the club — soon to be assisted by Mike Cook *(left)*. Mike, who was working at that time on *Farmers' Weekly* in Fleet Street, was a keen biker and had increasingly helped in the running of the club. Eventually he said he would like to work as full-time assistant to Graham so he went off to Leicester to do a crash course in youth work.'

When we interviewed Father Bill Shergold, now retired with his memories to Wells in Somerset, for this book he told us that he never re-visited the Ace after he left. 'The 59 Club just grew and grew and I even presented a petition to the Ministry of Transport in November 1966 to protest against the proposed raising of the minimum age for motorcycle licences from 16 to 17. In my view, it was inexperience, not age, which caused the accidents and I was in favour of better training. When Graham moved to another job, Mike took over the club and remained so until made redundant in July 1992 when the grant was withdrawn by the local council.'

The Twilight Years

Friday, late afternoon, the weekend traffic is just beginning its jammed and crawling flight from London. It's nothing like the bumper-to-bumper crush on an LA Freeway or on any of the expressways out of Philadelphia or New York. London streets don't much resemble those in the US cities. For one thing, what few expressways there are end way out on the periphery of the city. These streets are narrower and there are fewer cars. Because traffic lights aren't paced and many intersections have cops, driving is a block-to-block experience. On Friday night the lorries (trucks) are in a hurry to get back to their garages. For the summer weekend, everyone wants out of London.

We creep, sprint, stop, start again toward London's North Circular Road. In the States, we might call it a beltway, only it's much more primitive than that. Though at one time it was probably really outside the city's metropolitan sprawl, now it arches across a mile or two inside. Still, in a land of crazy-quilt streets and roads, the North Circular Road is about the only continuous path from the west of London to the northwest. There are two lanes in each direction, sometimes three, divided for the most part by an iron fence or a bit of grass or hedge. Some stretches go for as much as a mile without a stop, but there are frequent traffic lights and intersections. Lorry traffic is very heavy. Lorries from the industrial North circle about here to get a bead on their London destinations. Drivers on their way in and out of the city like to stop at diners or 'kaffs' as they call them to exchange road information and the woes shared by their kind.

We learn that distances as measured in terms of US cities are different here. Shorter, by and large, although metropolitan

London's nine million people occupy a large area. Maybe its because London's a financial and trade center rather than a manufacturing center. Somehow industry doesn't take up so much real estate, and quite beautiful homes line the side streets in downtown London. There is no abrupt transition from city to suburbs. Houses are everywhere. We get to the North Circular Road in about twenty minutes from Piccadilly Circus, the heart of the theater district.

Left on the NCR, left-hand side in the British fashion. We drive along until we spot the Ace Cafe on the eastbound lane. We swing in and park, noticing half-dozen bikers out front and several large tractor-trailer rigs. The watch shows 4.30 p.m. We are wearing tan raincoats and have been told in London that these are usually the costume of the fuzz.

Inside sit a handful of leather boys and their 'birds,' just like in the movies. The juke box is playing noisily but not much is happening. The room is quite small and we see a newly-added partition and door with a Lorry-Drivers-Club-Members-Only sign on it. There are places for maybe 40 people to sit down, and the drill is to get your tea and chips at the counter and take them to your seat. Seats and tables are bolted into place and are made of chrome and plastic and formica and the floor is a kind of institutional imitation-marble. The place has a cold feel to it and is moderately dirty.

A few of the leather jackets eye us suspiciously. We shuffle a bit, then go over to the counter for some watery coffee. We ask the counterman where all the motorcyclists are, feeling slightly idiotic. He tries to appraise us. 'They don't come here much anymore,' he says, dropping what has obviously become the management's line. 'We're from an American Bike magazine,' we say. 'Just want-

ed to ask some of the riders about the kinds of machinery they prefer over here.' The counterman considers this a minute then calls out, 'Hey, Terry.' A bearded fellow who has been watching the exchange stops munching greasy fries (chips). 'Coupla 'Merican chaps got some questions for ya.'

The word 'American' has some magic to these riders, but for the minute it means only 'not a cop.' Terry gets up and comes over, slowly. We tell him we're from an American bike magazine and are curious about the London bike scene. We talk at the counter for awhile, he very guardedly. We learn that he has a sidecar rig, and that its down for repair. We diagnose his problem as one of the transmission alignment and tell him what to do about it. This proves to be our true introduction and suddenly our tan raincoats and neckties don't matter anymore. The message is that we are motorcyclists.

'When I moved to Dover in 1969 I began a 69 Club and then a 79 Club (above) when I became rector of Tunstall, a small village near Sittingbourne, Kent, although I still remained Chairman of the original 59 Club. It had moved again to St. Augustine's, in Yorkton Street, Haggerston, in 1974 and to its present location in Plaistow in March 1993. Although today the club is but a shadow of what it was in my day, having only around 500 members . . . yet the spirit of those days 40 years ago still lives on at the new headquarters at the Swift Centre in the Barking Road (right).'

The girls and boys of the Ace now under the gaze of the Americans. Mavis and Doreen on the left

Terry names off a half-dozen other places frequented by the riders. The Busy Bee, another truck stop, about 15 miles out on the Watford bypass, looms as the largest. Then there's the Cellar, 16 miles due west in Windsor, a town known for Windsor Castle and Eton College. In north London, the Dug-out, a basement jukebox club, lies at the end of a tortuous alley. And in central London proper there's the 59 Club, run by two motorcycling clergymen. A few other places complete this small constellation of motorcycle hangouts, all within 30 miles of each other, and each likely to be visited in a single night's riding. On Friday and Saturday night, a thousand or more bikes may be plying this circuit.

Terry gets up. 'Got to go to work,' he says. 'You won't see much action here until maybe nine o'clock. Some night there are two hundred bikes here at a time. Some nights none at all.' We asked him what his job was. 'Diesel mechanic,' he says. 'I work nights with plenty of overtime. Make maybe twenty-five quid a week.' He is obviously proud of this sum,

We take our tepid coffee over to one of the bolted-down tables, get introduced, start talking bikes. Nearly all of these leather boys are younger than their American equivalents, ranging from about 17 to 22. At that age one can't conceal enthusiasm beneath caution very long. Soon we are overwhelmed with questions about cycling in America, about what kinds of machine we ride, what sort of modifications owners make to their bikes, what the American 'scene' is like. We answer, meanwhile trying to extract similar information from them.

The Ace Cafe, we learn, remains one of the major meeting places, despite the fact that two 'motorcycle' films have been shot there and innumerable press interviews conducted there during the brief era of Mods-versus-Rockers publicity. The Ace has the advantage of lying on the NCR and its relatively close into London compared with most other places on the circuit. The Ace offers easy entrance and exit and the rough informality of a truck stop. Outside, the NCR stands ready for any 'burn-off's' that arise during the nightly ritual of comparing motorcycles. The riders come mostly from the north of London, although several cruising parties during an evening will come from the south side of the city or from outlying towns. The Ace is a popular stopover.

Jack, Kenny, Jimmy and Roy . . . but big changes are on the way.

which comes to 75 US dollars. Britain's national average is about 14 pounds sterling a week, and most of these 'Rockers', working as apprentices at skilled trades or as laborers, earn between £14 and £20. Besides his side-car rig, Terry owns a big twin solo. He says about his pay, 'It's enough to keep me in bikes.'

We walk with him outside, followed by several other riders. A few bikes have come and gone since we arrived, but there are still fewer than a dozen machines. 'Come back tonight,' everyone tells us. They have begun to enjoy the attention shown them and right away blow most of their cool. Terry fired up and cuts into the fast, ragged traffic of the North Circular Road. We climb into our sedan and head for the nearest pub.

Our first impression of the motorcycles seen about the streets of London was how terribly old and ratty they were. Pre-war bikes can still be seen in working order, not as collectors' items but as daily transportation. Many other bikes from the 'fifties fall into this category. British weather does little to preserve machinery and all the commuters gave up polishing years ago. This doesn't hold, however, for the Rockers' bikes. Perhaps just as old as purely commuter bikes, they are almost always immaculate. With little cash to spend, a rocker's repairs may be crude, and parts from different machines will be fitted if they're cheap and in top running order.

Another thing we noticed about Rocker bikes is that they will only be 'stock' if brand new. Customizing at a rather primitive level is the absolute rule. First to go are the standard handlebars, which are replaced by clip-ons. Racing-type tank and seat are next. Then come modifications to the exhaust system, plus new paint and other minor decorating. The Rockers strive for a 'racer' image and so rarely hang superfluous goodies all over the machine. Neither do they do much about brake or engine modifications. We asked one rider why he hadn't put on a better set of brakes. 'There's not much can stop you from the ton, is there?' he answered. A full-house engine job on any of the big twins would be prohibitively expensive. Though it might shine in the 'burn offs', a bike is also used day-to-day where high reliability is essential. The aim is therefore to get the best possible performance from essentially stock engines. Since individuality is highly regarded, we saw many specials, such as Tibsas, Vinors, and Tritons.

In 1960, the Vincent Owners' Club highlighted how '. . . motorcycling was getting a particularly bad name from the Ace Cafe, ton-up, Rocker sensationalism that the press capitalised on . . .' but it was not until 1971 that legislation finally caught up with bike riders. That year, 16-year-olds were limited to riding mopeds only and safety helmets for all two-wheel riders were made compulsory in 1973. The 1980s saw the introduction of the two-part motorcycle test; a two-year restriction on the use of provisional licences, and learner motorcyclists limited to machines of 125 c.c., with compulsory basic training and a ban on learners carrying pillion passengers coming into force in 1990.

The unannounced but widely understood ritual of initiation into this brotherhood, we learned, is 'doin' the ton.' As one young rider told us, 'You have to do it once. Of course you don't ride around at 100 m.p.h. all the time, but its good to know you've done it, to know you bike can do it or once did it.' And they don't do the ton on a racecourse on a flat stretch of country road. Likely as not they do it on the North Circular Road, or the Watford bypass or the M1 (one of Britain's few limited access expressways). They don't do the ton in broad daylight when there's no traffic and the pavement is dry. Likely as not they do it at night, when challenged to burn-off (or burn-out). The air will be damp and the high beam won't be good for more than 60 m.p.h. and there will be trucks and cars of all sizes on the road. And that, mate, is when you do the ton. There has to be a story in it, for it will be told by a rider and his chums many times over. You have to make it good.

affair. Far fewer officers are assigned this chore than in the US, which makes driving or riding therefore a kind of lottery. The odds are against your getting caught so everybody speeds. As one of our group said: 'You'd be crazy to go the speed limit. Some lorry would flatten you from behind.' At night traffic is light and your pace brisk.

Charlie Williams went to school with Brian in Bushey. 'In 1946 I moved into the prefabs at Meadway, about a mile and a half from the Busy Bee,' recalls Charlie. 'In those days the Watford bypass was very countryfied. There was no speed limit, the traffic moved very fast, and there were no roundabouts, only a couple of crossroads. We used to go over to the cafe and see the people with their bikes when we were still at school and that gave me the idea that I would like a motorcycle myself when I was old enough. My first bike was an old Tiger 100 which I bought in 1959 when I was 16½ and I then started to go to the Busy Bee regularly with many of my schoolmates. Sadly the place closed down in 1968 and was knocked down for re-development. Fortunately the actual site of the Bee, behind me in the picture (below), remains landscaped beside the car park of the Hilton Hotel, and for reunions we have permission to dig a section out of the turf to expose the old floor tiles which are still there.'

'See you at the Bee.' Brian Jobson with his girlfriend Dawn from Borehamwood outside the Busy Bee.

That night we made the rounds of the motorcycle kaffs. We returned to the Ace just as a group was leaving for the Busy Bee. The air was dark and chilly. Leather jackets and Barbour suits were zipped up snugly. Two sidecar rigs rode with us and half a dozen solos. We cut into the heavy traffic immediately, motorcycle engines snarling angrily. A few miles of weaving and the group peeled off to the left and started cross-country on a winding in-town-and-out road. Traffic was light and we learned that a section of the north-south M1 had been opened almost to the NCR.

A group of three riders split off from us, yelling 'See you at the Bee.' Their screaming departure up a side road reminds us that traffic enforcement in Britain is a very random

'I also went to the Cherie caff in Borehamwood which used to be at No. 42 in the High Street and eventually I graduated to the Ace. I spent most of my time there — evenings and week-ends. In those days traffic was light and it only took about 20 minutes round the back roads to get to the Ace.

'I only had one accident which was when I went headlong into the Aldenham reservoir. I was distracted by a blonde from one of the film studios standing at the bus stop while I was going round the S-bend and I ran out of road and ended up in the water. (Shame! I never did see her again!)'

'My next bike was a 350cc Gold Star, followed by a Gold Star 500 which I was riding in 1962 when I was one of the extras in *The Leather Boys* film. We were employed on that for a week and, although the registration VLB 537 is not clear in these shots *(above)*, I am riding on the left not wearing a

helmet leading the pack out of the side entrance of the Ace. I then had a Matchless 500 G45 Racer before I changed to a Triumph Norton Manx Bonneville and later a Norton 600. I had two more Gold Stars, both 500s, and still have the last one that I bought from Doug Clark in New Southgate in 1966.'

We circle a roundabout and head down a long, very dark straight-away. We can dimly make out lights and the roar of traffic to our left — the M1 southern extension. Up ahead, a mile or two away, we see flashing blue light. Slowing down, we come upon an accident scene. A twisted motorcycle lies in the street amidst broken glass and large pools of dark liquid. The only light is from the headlight of the police car. Another car stands at an awkward angle near the curb and several figures are dimly visible standing about. Our group roars past, continues another mile, crests a slight rise and descends on the Busy Bee

For the leather boys, the Busy Bee offers everything. It stands as a super diner, all yellow tiles and furniture of metal tubing. Once a large truck stop, it too has been bypassed by the M1 extension. There are acres of parking lot, perfect dramatic entrances and exits and for minor horseplay. Then there's the Watford bypass, a road that bypasses the town of Watford and that has now been bypassed by the M1. There it is — more than two miles of lightly traveled straight-away, perfect for burn-outs and for doing the ton. The Busy Bee, now that the lorry drivers no longer stop, has become a late-night refreshment spot for the young people from surrounding communities. the majority are cyclists, but many show up in cars. Among that second group are the Mods.

Now the Mods of Mods-vs-Rockers fame observe a considerable different lifestyle than the Rockers, though they come from the same 16-to-early-20s age group. Where most Rockers are tradesmen or laborers, most Mods are white-collar workers-clerks in any of the enormous bureaucracies that British society produces.

The dress of the Mods is stylish, modish (or 'mod'), colorful, expensive, and carefully maintained. For transportation, the Mods have chosen motor-scooters, mostly Vespas and Lambrettas, which, again are more stylish or stylized than most motorcycles, and to which they add a vast array of lights, reflectors, horns and mirrors. Scootering has a functional value: the machines are cleaner and therefore protect the rider and his prized clothing from road grime as well as engine grime. Mod hangouts or meeting places are more often coffee-houses than diners and cafes.

These clearly distinguishable differences between groups of young people make for clearly defined conflict, especially in a society

In this 1964 picture, taken inside the Busy Bee, Charlie Williams has his back to the camera on the extreme left. Other bikers recognisable are 'Bogey', Johnny Clark, 'Biggen', 'Re-bore Ray', Kenny Knight, 'Spud' and 'Doddy'. Two years later the Bee's lasting claim to fame was confirmed when it was featured in the film which established Michael Caine as a major film star. *Alfie* was an immense success and it also immortalised Charlie who appeared in it sitting at a table by the window: 'My nickname was "Polo" because I was always sucking "the mint with a hole" so most people knew me as Charlie Polo.'

as class-oriented as modern Britain. Mods versus Rockers means clerk versus laborer, white-collar versus blue-collar, dude versus scrub, scooterist versus cyclist, dandy versus tough. A few rumbles at beach resorts and there's a beautiful bit of puffery for the international press.

The flaw in such journalism is that the class origins of these young people are really not all that distinct. They all come from lower or lower-middle class families. Their respective incomes are about the same. Besides turning on to girls and music, they (like the papers say) all go to the beach. Probably more girls flock to the Mod crowd, because fashion and artiness conventionally have more feminine appeal.

At the Busy Bee we saw just about how the group conflict works out — what the rules of the game are. Everyone accepts that the Busy Bee is primarily a Rocker watering

place. So when the Mods show up, they must divest themselves of their most conspicuous symbol. This season the symbol is a kind of poncho or cape that pulls over one's head and substitutes for a jacket. Rainbow colors and exotic weaves create a flamingo effect Mod males leave their capes in the cars when they come into the Busy Bee. Women don't count in the battle, and the girls from either group come in dressed as they are. For the most part, the Mods and their girls sit apart in a group by themselves, rather stiffly. In a Rocker stronghold, they don't push their luck, and the Rockers usually leave them alone. The cyclists by contrast are spirited, playful, energetic and assertive.

No scooters are parked among the rows of bikes outside the Busy Bee. While the scooterists is inside, minor mishaps might occur to his ride, like getting knocked over, mysteriously dented, or otherwise abused.

Then and now outside the Bee with the A41 beyond.

Conversely, if a group of Rockers (and its always a group) should enter a Mod coffeehouse, they sit by the window within view of their machines. Mods are not unknown to pour a little sugar into a motorcycle gastank, pull out spark plug leads or deflate tires.

Very occasionally there actually is a 'punch up,' but its usually between individuals rather groups. And what kills it as news is the fact that British young people are just too civilized to badly hurt one another. Fights are stopped by the others when one party has been bested. 'Fair play' actually means something in the nation that created the concept. If anything impressed us about the Mods and Rockers it was how considerate they were, toward their own and toward their opponents. No murders, no rapes, no frenzied sadistic beatings . . . just an occasional 'row.'

Within the Rocker group itself lies more evidence of this kind of consideration. At the Busy Bee there is a kind of bulletin board where messages are left about injured or ill members of the group. Collections are taken for the family of a rider killed or badly injured in an accident. Parents are notified when one of the group is in some kind of trouble. Riders lend one another parts and tools and almost always stop to help a stalled rider by the roadside, whether they know him or not. Many riders also belong to volunteer emergency blood service. They carry whole-blood or plasma from hospitals and bloodbanks to various points about London, or even, in relay teams, to places in the distant countryside. 'The law won't touch ya when you're savin' somebody's bloody life,' one rider laughed.

Drinking, in a land where there's a pub in every neighborhood if not on every corner, is largely avoided by the Rockers. They live too close to the road, too close to the memory of recent accidents. In the rare instances when a group does stop for a pint or two, they will notice when one of their numbers has had too much. Many a 'stolen' machine has been ridden safely home by a rider's mate while others distracted his tipsy friend.

Beside the nightly round on the cafe circuit, Rockers occasionally organize what they call a weekend 'burn-up.' This takes the form of a fast cross-country ride to some point in the north of England or to Wales or Scotland. Within 60 miles of London lie the Brighton resort area and the Snetterton and Brands Hatch racecourses. These are too close for an all-out burn-up, and more appropriate destinations are Liverpool or Manchester or even Edinburgh (470 miles). Trips take two days, possibly with a layover at a friendly club or possibly straight through. We asked the riders in our group how their bikes held up under such grueling conditions (until recently there was no speed limit at all on the open road in Britain).

We had finished making the rounds of the Rocker cafes and clubs by 2.30 a.m. or so. By then the groups were breaking up, the riders heading for home and all but the truck stops closing for the night. The riders had made us welcome especially after learning that we also were bike people and weren't out for another big publicity smear. We left feeling that whatever excitement the rocker's life contains, its mostly the excitement of two wheels. He enjoys the companionship of his fellows, but friendships are mostly superficial and changing. Life as a Rocker lasts only a few years, for most will marry and gradually become involved in the responsibilities and interests of middle age. The oldest Rocker we met was 26, and he had the distinction of owning a Triumph 500 that could outrun the 650's..

London's leather boy is trapped in a tightly structured world, in a country with an economy that's at best static, in a society that promises him little social or economic advance. He hasn't many outlets for self expression and he feels a lot of anger. It's little wonder that he turns to two wheels. 'When you've got no place to go, mate, you go fast,' one rider told us. Perhaps the prospect of death is not so frightening from such a perspective. Those who are outside the Rocker world don't understand. They call the Rocker a tough guy . . . and so might those who do understand.

An American view by John P. Covington

145

Resurrection

The Ace is dead. England's most notorious transport café — once a teenage motor-cyclists' Mecca — has closed.

Now the only two-wheelers to pull up on its oil-stained tarmac forecourt off London's North Circular Road are those waiting to be fitted with tyres at the depot which has opened on the site.

The scarred metal tables and the most uncomfortable chairs ever designed, which withstood the onslaughts of the original coffee-bar cowboys, saw the coming of the ton-up kids, and outlasted the era of the rocker, have been torn out to make way for stacks of tyres.

Branded by TV and the press as a haunt of the motorcycling drop-out, the Ace was more of a modern Pickwick Club where friends would meet and tell tales of daring-do. Of near brushes with the law, of the speeds around Neasden's 'Suicide Bridge' and of the never-to-be-believed best times from the forecourt to the rival café, the Busy Bee at Watford.

The worn jukebox has gone. In its time it was fed a fortune, often kicked, sometimes used as a bet settler. Many was the wager that revolved around how far a rider could get up the North Circular and back before a disc stopped playing.

But those were the days before the bulk of the Circular Circuit was enveloped in the mass 40 m.p.h. restrictions of a few years ago. The speed limit was the first nail in the Ace coffin.

Police, never reluctant to investigate the customers closely, paid even more attention to the speeds achieved by the riders and, eventually, the café became the in-place to avoid.

Time was when 100 bikes lined up every evening in ragged order outside the brick-built temple. In its last days, a handful at the Ace was a crowd.

Press report, 1969

The Ace finally closed in 1969 . . . a victim of changing times . . . and values. More practical use was found for the building which was converted into a tyre-fitting depot, this aerial oblique being taken in 1978.

From 1979 . . . to 1994! A major reconstruction and realignment of the North Circular between Harrow Road and Hangar Lane fortunately led to the old road, on the left in this picture, being retained to service the industrial and business properties on the northern side — including the Ace.

Formidable traffic problems exist within the north-west sector of the A406 between Hangar Lane and east of Harrow Road. With an average daily traffic flow of 60,000 vehicles in 1983 and 70,000 in 1990, this section of the North Circular Road was classified as the 8th busiest road in London.

The scheme has been designed as a 50mph (80kph) all purpose dual three-lane carriageway road. Two grade separated junctions have been provided; one at Park Royal and the other at the junction with Harrow Road.

The scheme has four road bridges, seven rail bridges, two foot bridges, two pedestrian subways, an aqueduct carrying the Grand Union Canal, and a box culvert to accommodate a local stream. Some 1600 metres of retaining walls with a maximum height of approximately 8 metres are also incorporated into the scheme to retain cuttings at underpasses and the British Rail bridges.

The diversion of the multitude of the services located along the scheme and at the major crossing at Harrow Road, was a substantial task in itself. Approximately ten services companies were involved and close liaison was necessary to avoid delays to the contracts. One major diversion in particular; that of British Telecom, had to be located in a tunnel under the NCR to avoid such a problem.

The decks of all rail bridges were designed to be built alongside the rail track and were moved into position over week-end closures of the railway. The abutments of the British Rail bridges were thurst bored and jacked into position under the railway lines whilst the tracks were in use.

The Grand Union Canal could only be closed for a limited period so the aqueduct was constructed to one side and moved into position during the canal closure period.

The majority of the retaining walls are of contiguous bored pile construction with a stabilising base to avoid the need for temporary works.

Highways Agency, November 1994

Some half a million cubic metres had to be shifted by Edmund Nuttalls Ltd from the mound of Blitz rubble opposite the Ace to make way for the new road. This spoil was removed by rail between September 1989 and August 1990.

Now consigned to a backwater, the new road spelled the end of the old Lex garage

Barry took this shot of his old abandoned race-track on the southbound carriageway.

ROCKIN' AT THE ACE CAFE

Well, dig the sound, shakin' the ground
  burnin' up the carriageway
Dig the sound of a big 650
Super Rocket BSA
Hot on the tail of a shiny black Bonneville
  headin' for the Ace Cafe

Jimmy come ridin' the black Bonneville
  got a jacket of studded leather
When Jimmy come walkin' in the Ace Cafe
  you'd think there was a change in the weather
Got his eyes wide open for a fast lookin' girl
  you can bet they'll be leavin' together

Ridin', ridin', ridin' to the Ace Cafe
Ridin' ridin' ridin' to the Ace Cafe
On a black Bonneville and a Super Rocket BSA

Ricky looks cool in a long red jacket
  with a jet black velvet lapel
Got a bootlace tie, tight black jeans
  and white beetle-crushers as well
Dancin' with Julie to the juke-box rhythm
  of The King singin' Heartbreak Hotel

Red head Julie, turned sixteen
  decided she could live on her own
That's what she said to her father and mother
  when she told 'em she was leavin' home

She said "No need to worry, I've saved up my money
  if I need anymore I'll 'phone"

Red head Julie, turned sixteen today
She's dressed to kill, ready to be on her way
Lookin' for action, she found it at the Ace Cafe

When Julie hit town, she wandered around
  lookin' for a place to stay
Then a teenage Rocker on a souped-up Tiger Cub
  took her to the Ace Cafe
He thought he would score, but then Ricky hit the floor
  and stole Julie's heart away

Jet black Jimmy stuck his glass on the jukebox
  threw his cigarette on the floor
Then he walked up to Rick, who was boppin' so slick
  and pointed out the way to the door
Ricky turned 'round slow, said "Boy, you'd better blow,
I've flattened better cats than you before"
Call the cops on the double, there's trouble at the Ace Cafe
Hear the waiter grumble, there's a rumble at the Ace Cafe
Well, I can't deny it there's a riot at the Ace Cafe

Julie got wise, tears in her eyes
  she was wishin' she was back at home
She shouted "Go on fightin' just as long as you like,
I'd be better off on my own"
Ricky and Jimmy stood starin' at each other
  while Julie walked away alone

She pulled a scarf on her head and ran out into the pourin'
  rain
Then she hitched a ride on a wagon and was gone again
  bumpin' and rollin' back home on the Northbound lane

And they kept on rockin', rockin', rockin' at the Ace Cafe
Rockin', rockin', rockin' at the Ace Cafe
Rockin', rockin' at the Ace Cafe

Ridin', ridin', ridin to the Ace Cafe
Ridin' ridin', ridin' to the Ace Cafe
On a black Bonneville and a Super Rocket BSA.

WORDS AND MUSIC © MARTIN CRAIG, 1973

Yet memories of the great days at the Ace lived on, not only in the minds of those who were there at the time but in those of a new breed of motorcyclists. Martin Craig was 15 when he first visited the Ace: 'I went there during a day on my own in London whilst my father was on business. I'd seen it in the *Dixon of Dock Green* programme and read about the Ace in *John Bull* magazine which had published a full photo and text feature in fairly sensational terms. I was overwhelmed by my visit which was pretty intimidating to a 15-year-old, but incredibly exciting. Even then I could see the difference between the Ace and the average transport caff and that inspired me to set the legend of the Ace to music in *Rockin' at the Ace Cafe* which I wrote in 1973.' But what else could be done to bring those great days back?

For decades the Ace Cafe was the round-the-clock meeting point for motorcycle enthusiasts.

Yesterday, 25 years after its closure, the forecourt reverberated to the roar of the Triumph Bonneville, the Norton 500 and the 'Beezer' as about 5,000 bikers returned to relive the halcyon days of the cafe at Stonebridge Park on the North Circular Road at Wembley.

The passage of time has seen many one-time tearaways settle down to respectable family life. Much of the British motorcycle

One man's vision made it all come true . . . but it was not to happen overnight. In 1994, Mark Wilsmore approached Just Tyres to ask if he could take the place over for a day to celebrate the 25th anniversary of the closure of the Ace. The event was successful beyond his wildest dreams.

industry has also gone and, to the regret of many, Japanese machines were much in evidence during the reunion.

It was a day to recall the 'Ton-Up Boys' of the early 1950s who — thanks to the wonders of hire purchase — were able to afford and race machines which would otherwise have been beyond their reach.

By the 1960s the 'Ton-Up Boys' had been supplanted by the Rockers. 'It was all about having fun on the bikes,' Colin Pryce-Jones said. 'It was never about taking drugs, it was the Mods and later the hippies who used to pop pills.'

The Daily Telegraph, September 5, 1994

A leather-clad throng converged from all points of the compass on London's North Circular Road for the *Classic Bike*-Ace Cafe reunion. Police estimates of 5,000 bikes, and up to double that number of people, probably weren't far out, but who could tell? The only certain thing is this was the biggest classic bike meeting of the year by some margin.

Organiser Mark Wilsmore reported a feeling of great pride as he surveyed the wall of leather and steel from a vantage point above the old Ace Cafe building, now a Just Tyres depot. The turnout surprised him, us and everyone we spoke to.

Father Scott Anderson, figurehead of the world famous 59 Club, gave a short service to remember absent friends who diced and lost on the treacherous orbital road. And bands played throughout the day at the Abbey pub, 500 yards anti-clockwise from the Ace.

But it wasn't the pub, or even the bikes that was the focus of the event. It was the people. Reminiscence hung strong in the air as former Ace goers met up with friends not seen for thirty years. And the new wave of ton-up boys got a chance to chat with their forbears.

Classic Bike, October 1994

As Mark surveyed the scene from the roof top, the view was incredible for not only was the car park jam-packed but the roads outside were thronged with upwards of 5,000 bikes.

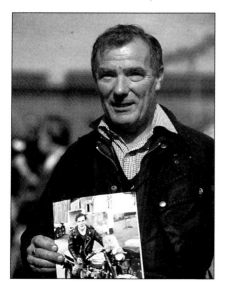

Noddy was there and many of his old mates like Don Budd, Cecil Richards (see page 114), Doug Budd and Charlie Williams.

The tremendous response was amazing as it demonstrated to Mark just how much the Ace meant to bikers of all ages and it set him on a quest which was to occupy his every waking hour for the next seven years. His ultimate goal was to secure the Ace and restore it back to what it once was — a cafe for what he describes as 'petrolheads'. But meanwhile he set about holding annual 'Ace Days'. Three years later he was in a position to use the annexe on the side which had once been the posh part of the original cafe. And appropriate signage denoted its weekend opening.

A legendary bikers' cafe which fed egg and chips to rock legends for most of the 1950s and '60s could rise, phoenix-like, from the ashes if planning permission is agreed. But among the opponents of the plans to recreate the old Ace Cafe will be its current occupants, Just Tyres.

Visionary enthusiast Mark Wilsmore, who lives in Hendon, hopes to recreate the Ace on its original site beside the North Circular in Wembley, 27 years after the original Rockers' pilgrimage site closed.

He has not revealed who will foot the bill for the £1 million development — which still has to overcome the tricky problem of how to accommodate the tyre company. But he hopes to revive the golden days of British rock'n'roll with a dance hall, memorial hall, cafe and sandwich bars which will give today's teenagers a flavour of the heyday of Cliff Richard, Johnny Kidd and the Pirates, Tommy Steele, Billy Fury and even the Beatles.

'It will not be a nostalgia trip or a museum,' he said. 'It will be an attempt to recreate a crucial cultural period which has profound significance today. I hope it will appeal to many of the people who originally came here — and also to today's teenagers. It may sound crass but I believe it is almost as much a part of our heritage as the Tower of London.

'There has been such enormous interest in the old cafe that I feel a great responsibility to do it properly,' said Mark.

Architect John Massey was chosen to plan the project after Mark had met a friend of his in a Notting Hill pub and, Mark says: 'He seemed to have understood instantly what I wanted to do — he has a soul.'

Other celebrity visitors during the cafe's 31-year existence included Johnny Briggs, *Coronation Street*'s Mike Baldwin; The Who bassist John Entwhistle; American pop star Gene Vincent; and, it is thought, actress Diana Dors. John Lennon and Paul McCartney in their Quarrymen days, are thought to have been thrown out as they were writing a song because they played a Buddy Holly track so many times on the jukebox.

Celebrated motorcycle racers such as Ray Pickeral, Dave Goddard and Dave Degens also began their racing from the cafe with its legendary Ton-Up Boys, whose speciality was ignoring the speed limit.

But Just Tyres management has dismissed the plan. A spokesman said: 'The site is not for sale. We have not received a formal offer from any interested party.'

Wembley Observer, November 1996

The momentous day dawned. The Council Offices are only 15 minutes ride away, but I checked the bike over to make sure I got there. The meeting commenced at 7.30 p.m. I had plenty of time to reflect on the four years work to date, involving architects, surveyors, engineers and many other professionals. Tonight's meeting was with the Planning Committee — without their consent, nothing could happen!

Riding there alone, I was apprehensive, having done so much, still I was finding myself wondering if it was enough. Had we overlooked anything? We were entirely dependent on the outcome of this meeting, but I focused my mind on the support I had been shown. Cutting through the evening traffic along North Circular Road, it occurred to me that of course they would give us the go ahead: this is unique . . . this is the ACE!

I arrived early with time to spare and found my way to the Council Chambers. Surrounded by people in suits, I felt very conscious of being the only person in the room in black leather. Hundreds of eyes looked in my direction from faces that told me to keep quiet. Numerous applications were dealt with on a wide range of different topics, progress was slow. When would our application be heard?

I dare not move, my leathers were noisy. If I went out for a smoke, I may miss it. So I sat tight. After three hours, the clerk announced: 'Ace Cafe'. I sat up straight whilst everyone was looking at me. The clerk continued with a solemn voice 'change of use' and all he said sounded so technical, so unimportant, giving me a feeling that our case already was to be dropped.

The chairman of the committee welcomed me. 'Well,' he said, 'it's the ACE, right, we've already gone through the case, haven't we, Ladies and Gentleman.' He looked around to his colleagues, the Councillor stating: 'We want this. A piece of our heritage. I'm for it.' There was no debate, just a clear unanimous decision, YES!

I could not get out of there fast enough, my leather boots slipping on the polished marble floor. I kicked the bike into life, grinning from ear to ear, feeling the adrenalin pumping through me. I took a detour past the ACE, with one thought, WE CAN DO IT NOW!! Yes, we have made it. We got the planning permission, and ACE CAFÉ LONDON has now bought the original Ace Cafe site.

Mark Wilsmore, January, 1997

At its meeting on January 16, 1997 the Planning Committee of the London Borough of Brent gave the go-ahead for the change of use from a tyre depot. Now for Mark (right) it was full steam ahead.

Hundreds of merry motorcylists from all over the world flocked to London to celebrate the recent reopening of the famous Ace Cafe, 28 years after its closure.

The historic moment was shared by former regulars and curious newcomers to the meeting spot on London's North Circular Road.

Following the official reopening, site owner Mark Wilsmore served visitors a cup of English tea to mark the occasion. The Ace Cafe will now open every Sunday until the summer as Wilsmore gears up towards full-time operation.

'Reopening the cafe has been a long-time dream of mine. It is an important part of British biking history,' he said.

The Daily Telegraph, December 13, 1997

Mark devoted the first Wednesday evening of each month specially for American vehicles and a wide variety gathered on the forecourt . . . from saloons . . . to sports coupes . . . to customised street racers.

London, England — 'See you at the Ace,' says Mark Wilsmore kicking his Triton into life. The tea in our cups spills over and seconds later the London rush hour has devoured the founder of the Ace Cafe Reunion. He's in a hurry, as usual, since he founded the Ace Cafe Reunion five years ago. Mark's goal is to reopen London's legendary Ace Cafe. The Rockers met there, listened to rock n' roll and burned up the road doing The Ton (100mph) — the magic speed — through the city streets of London. They were daring and dangerous.

Driven by a passion for motorbikes and rock n'roll, Mark Wilsmore started planning in 1993 to reopen the legendary cafe..

Since then major steps have been made towards the reopening of the Ace Cafe, including securing the original site and launching the Ace Cafe Club, with parts of the original Ace Cafe opened to the public on Fridays, Saturdays and Sundays and on Bank Holidays and every first Wednesday of every month. Visitors can check out the place and see the progress. Based on the rich heritage and traditions of the 50's and 60's, the Ace Cafe still embodies the same value as when the original Rockers called it home. What could be found on a Triton going for the Ton in the sixties today can be found on a modern sportbike or streetfighter. The bikes, the music, and perhaps the whole world have changed, but the spirit remains the same: Non-conformist, rebellious, individual and authentic.

Motorcycle, March 18, 1998

THE ONE STOP (ROCKERS) SHOP

ACE CAFE LONDON

NOW OPEN FOR TEA CHIPS AND LEATHER

Ace Corner, North Circular Road, Stonebridge, London NW10

EVERY FRI 8pm-12pm

EVERY SAT Noon-12pm

EVERY SUN 8am-8pm (OPEN 'TIL MIDNIGHT WHEN FOLLOWED BY A BANK HOLIDAY MONDAY)

BANK HOLIDAY MONDAYS 10am-8pm

FIRST WEDNESDAY OF EVERY MONTH 7pm-12pm

ACE CAFE CLUB
To be a part of it, write to the address below or call in. You will make it happen!

ACE CAFE CLUB

Severe flooding caused mayhem on the North Circular Road after a water main burst on Saturday. As tailbacks stretched well into Hendon, the section of road between Hangar Lane and Harrow Road was submerged in up to 30 feet of water.

The flooding was caused by London's principle water main bursting under the road's surface on Sunday night.

Mark Wilsmore, 42, the owner of Ace Cafe, Ace Corner on the North Circular Road, Hendon, said: 'Myself and one other person were in the car park late at night. We heard whooshing sounds and as we were thinking: "What on earth?" by the time we'd thought "earth" the car park was standing up in front of me.

'All the asphalt was rising up. All I could see was the car park standing up and the bikes falling over and this plume of water shoot up. I have no idea how high. It just went up into the sky.'

All the water had been pumped from the scene by Tuesday and the road re-opened to traffic.

Hendon and Finchley Times, March 11,1999

Then in 1999 came disaster when the pipe carrying London's main water supply, which ran beneath the car park, suddenly burst on March 6. The fracture was a major one which flooded the North Circular to a depth of several feet. The tyre depot was underwater and it was touch and go as to whether the building was irrepairably damaged.

Fortunately it was not and, after a massive clear up, the Rockers shop re-opened.

Motorcyclists will have no excuse for not knowing where to go on Sundays this autumn as several new cafes open for business

Building plans for the renewed Ace Cafe on London's North Circular have gone to tender. The famous cafe was almost destroyed by a burst water main last year and owner Mark Wilsmore has ambitious plans to build a new Ace on the site of the old one.

'I think this tender business will involve a fair bit of negotiation,' he says, 'but I predict that we should be open by Christmas.' Until then, the Ace Cafe continues from a Portakabin on site, opening Friday nights, Saturday and Sunday and the first Wednesday of every month

The Daily Telegraph, August 12, 2000

By the middle of 2001, conversion — or should one say re-conversion — work was well under way. Meanwhile, the shop was temporarily installed in a Portakabin in the car park. July 4 — US Independent Day — was celebrated with an outdoor disco.

The famous Ace Cafe has finally come to the end of its refurbishment, and the official Grand Opening is almost upon us! This north London landmark has been hosting car, bike and Rock'n'Roll nights for the last few months, but they're finally ready to open full-time, with a five-day party planned for early September.

Things start off on Wednesday, September 5th, when the Executioners car club have their Flamin' Ace Riot, with all low-riders, customs, classics and hot-rods welcome. Thursday 6th is the March of the Mods, whilst Friday is Weekend Warm-Up Night featuring Steve Hooker & the STs, and Graham Fenton's tribute to Gene Vincent. Saturday 8th is the All-Day Party with the Best of British Bike Show, and the music goes on late into the night before Sunday's Ace Cafe Reunion with the ride-out to Brighton leaving at 9.30 in the morning!

Classic American, September 2001

Bikes fitted the image — the driving beat of rock 'n' roll in motion — and black leather gear looked pretty neat into the bargain. Before long anyone young who rode a motorcycle and wore leather jacket and jeans (eminently practical motorcycling gear) posed a threat to the British way of life.

In reality the behaviour of the motor-cyclists of the period was, in the main, extremely mild indeed. The majority were more than happy simply to spend the evening down the 'caff', in the company of their mates, spinning yarns about the bikes they couldn't afford and the girls they'd never met except in their imagination.

Life revolved around the caff. Pubs in those days (and these days) didn't welcome leather-jacketed bike riders with open arms. They upset the regular clientele, attracted the unwanted attention of the police and woke up the neighbours at stop-tap. The caff was where everything happened. It was warm and inviting and, best of all, it was cheap. With practice, you could avoid the watchful eye of the owner and make a cup of expresso coffee last an eternity. The time was spent chatting to mates or chatting up the birds who would hang around hoping to cadge a ride. Wherever you went there was always somebody you knew, somebody to talk bikes with. It was magic.

Bikers, Maz Harris, 1985

Then . . . and now. A few days before the official launch celebrations began, the doors of the new Ace swung open for business.

They've been told the story . . . and they've seen the film. *Right:* **Now these two young up-and-coming leather boys tuck** into their burgers where their forebears — for real *(left)* or for a film recreation *(top)* — scoffed their tea and chips.

Of all the Rocker haunts up and down the country the strongest and most impelling myths and legends were always associated with the Ace Cafe on London's North Circular. In the heady days of 1962 it was something to see the assembled line-up of bikes. Regulars were hooked on the excitement of watching machines screaming past.

In the days before 1965 when the police slapped on a speed limit of 70 and then 40 m.p.h. the din went on all night. Kids lined the pavement, stood on the parapet wall or even leaned out from the island in the middle of the dual carriageway just to watch the fun; it was better than any organised race track!

Bike thieving it is true went on at the Ace and there was a fair lot of trouble, although at the first stage of it, if so much as a coffee cup was broken, the manager would get on his hot line to Wembley Nick and the 'Old Bill' would come down.

Rockers, Johnny Stuart, 1987

PRESS RELEASE

ACE CAFE LONDON

It's in Britain and it's in London
The World's Most Famous Cafe
THE ACE CAFE is RE-OPENING
The original North Circular Road cafe restaurant and venue

GRAND OPENING WEEKEND STARTS

Wed.5th Sept. FLAMIN' ACE RIOT! with the EXECUTIONERS
Lowbrow Lowriders, Kool Kustoms, Krazy Klassics and Hot Rods

Thur.6th Sept. MARCH OF THE MODS!
My Generation - High Numbers Night

Fri.7th Sept. WEEKEND WARM UP NIGHT
Featuring Steve Hooker & The ST's, plus Rockabilly Rebel Graham Fenton's
tribute to Gene Vincent. Hot Wax courtesy of Mouse and Mad Dog Johnny B.

Sat.8th Sept. ALL DAY PARTY
Best of British Bike Show
Late Night With The Leather Boys & Girls!
Featuring The Johnson Family, Johnny Fox & The Hunters, plus DJ's Wild Wax &
Mad Dog Johnny B, with special guests to include Father Scott Anderson of 59 Club,
Faster Pastor Paul Sinclair and Rita Tushingham, star of the film The Leather Boys!

Sun.9th Sept. ACE CAFE REUNION
RIDE WITH THE ROCKERS leaves the cafe at 09.30
for ACE DAY BRIGHTON

**Ace Cafe London,
Ace Corner, North Circular Road, Stonebridge,
London, NW10 7UD**

OPEN 7 DAYS - 6am to 2am Fully Licensed

**Tel/Fax: 020 8961 1000
Website: www.ace-cafe-london.com**

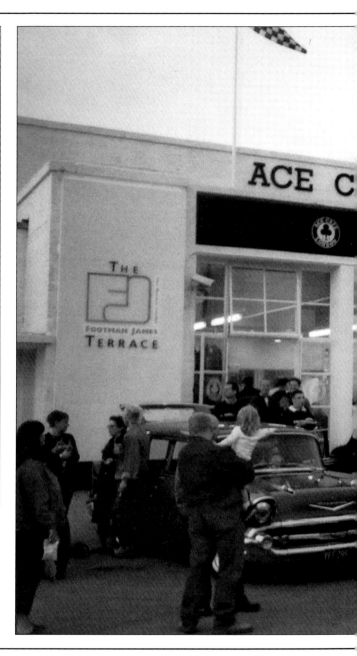

And so to the grand opening — with something for everyone! Linda Wilsmore, Editor of the *Ace Club Magazine*: 'When the historic day finally dawned, it is difficult to describe how we felt, having worked on the project for seven years. Apprehensive, elated, relieved? — all those and more! But overall was a sense of great achievement, which without your support and generosity in joining the club, through to the hands-on help over the years, may never have happened.' The celebrations stretched over five days, blessed with glorious summer sunshine. Kicking things into gear on the Wednesday were the Yanks.

The Ace lives, once again! The proceedings were watched over by both American and British police!

Thursday was the March of the Mods. They would never have dared to enter the Ace then . . . but now, with their scooters parked alongside the bikes, it was all mates together! (Come back Joe Loss. All is forgiven!)

Get yer kicks at the A406 um das Ace Cafe.

German website, 2001

At the *Classic Bike* sponsored official reopening on Saturday, September 8, thousands of Ace fans attended including celebrities Rita Tushingham, Colin Campbell, Jess Conrad, Mickey Most, Mike Sarne, and Wee Willie Harris.

Looking slightly fatigued but happy having finally achieved his ambition to make the Ace rev again, Mark Wilsmore, rather hoarse of voice, accepted the plaudits for his vision and dogged determination.

At 2.50 p.m. three cheers were heartily raised for Mark, the man who has resurrected the cult Ace Cafe.

Classic Bike, November 2001

Friday night . . . and Saturday morning! No sooner had the sounds of the evening's jam session by Steve Hooker and the STs — with Taka giving her rendering of the Wilson Pickett classic *Mustang Sally* — faded away, then a new sound was heard . . .

. . . the sound of hundreds of throbbing motors as the bikes roared up to the Ace for the big day.

Exactly 40 years after the massive police crack-down, both the boys in blue and those in black celebrated the re-opening.

It was a day of relived memories and sheer nostalgia . . . held against the backdrop of the famous series of rail bridges.

Above: The Leather Boys in the 1960s and *(below)* the leather boys — and girls — of the 21st century.

The test of time . . . then and now! Forty years later, the forecourt of the Ace echoes to the sounds of days long ago.

When the *Daily Herald* was transmogrified into the *Sun* (the original broadsheet version, not to-day's tabloid) the change was heralded by an immense advertising campaign which used the slogan 'Born of the age we live in'. It is a pretentious phrase, and the campaign was hardly a roaring success, but in some circles the slogan has survived as a catchphrase, almost invariably quoted sarcastically just as that other famous newspaper slogan (pinched from Henry James) is used: 'All human life is there'.

Yet when both phrases came into my mind last week, it was without any overtones of irony. Not wishing to watch soccer, golf, repeats of Parkinson interviews or a repeat of a Common Market documentary on the BBC channels, I turned instead to ITV's showing of Sidney Furie's 1964 movie *The Leather Boys*. When this was first shown in the cinema I was working as a film critic and I don't remember being very impressed, yet watching it for a second time, 10 years later, I was amazed to see how well it had withstood a whole decade of change.

Chris Dunkley, September 1974

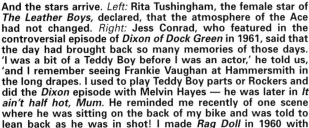

And the stars arrive. *Left:* Rita Tushingham, the female star of *The Leather Boys,* declared, that the atmosphere of the Ace had not changed. *Right:* Jess Conrad, who featured in the controversial episode of *Dixon of Dock Green* in 1961, said that the day had brought back so many memories of those days. 'I was a bit of a Teddy Boy before I was an actor,' he told us, 'and I remember seeing Frankie Vaughan at Hammersmith in the long drapes. I used to play Teddy Boy parts or Rockers and did the *Dixon* episode with Melvin Hayes — he was later in *It ain't half hot, Mum.* He reminded me recently of one scene where he was sitting on the back of my bike and was told to lean back as he was in shot! I made *Rag Doll* in 1960 with Hermoine Baddeley and Kenneth Griffiths and *Kil 1* with Ronald Howard in 1962. I was familiar with the Ace before we filmed there. I don't know whether it was because it was one of the first places with a jukebox or whether it was just somewhere that we could make a noise. Anyway we were all attracted there for the birds. The incredible thing was that one week I was a struggling actor and the next a pop star. After I became an overnight success with *Mystery Girl*, one of the incredible things was to play my own record on the jukebox at the Ace. I changed my old Hillman Minx for a mauve and white Ford Zodiac and we used to stop at the Ace on the way up north to gigs with Billy Fury and all the others.'

NORMAN TO JOYCE

JOYCE: Hello?

NORMAN (*very friendly*): Hello love, it's me.

JOYCE (*Not pleased to hear from him*): What do you want?

NORMAN: Well, look, we're going to be grandparents. Come on, let's bury the hatchet.

JOYCE: There's only one place I'd like to bury a hatchet.

MVO: Always on the phone? Well reconnect with BT Talk Together for just £14.99 a month including line rental, and get all your local evening and weekend calls for free.

NORMAN: Let me take you out for a meal. You know they've re-opened the Ace Café.

JOYCE (*Softening a bit*): But you haven't got a motorbike any more.

NORMAN: Better than that. I've got an Austin Allegro (*they both start laughing*).

MVO (*Over reprise of signature tune*): Free local calls are yet another reason to reconnect for free. Call 0800 XXX XXX. That's 0800 XXX XXX. BT bringing . . .

NORMAN: Norman

MVO: and

JOYCE: Joyce

MVO: together

BT Advertisement, 2001

One nice feature in the restored cafe is the 'Wall of Fame' where notable personalities — from then and now — can sign in.

Meanwhile, outside entertainment was provided by a variety of bands including the Johnson Family, Johnny Fox and the Hunters, the Carlo Little All Stars and vocalists Alan Barrett, Johnny Casanova, Wee Willie Harris and Mike Sarne.

Most important of all were the stars of yesteryear . . . those who were there and helped create the legend: as they were . . . and as they are today. *Above left:* Tony 'Wig' Evans.

Above right:. **Barry 'Noddy' Cheese with Maggie Spalding (née Gurhy).** *Below left:* **Yvonne Williams** and *(below right)* **Charlie Williams (no relation) on his first Gold Star.**

It's yesterday once more. Reunion at the Ace after 40 years. L-R: Tony, Maggie, Barry, Yvonne and Charlie.

Tony: 'I lost my girlfriend through this place. I thought the world of her but her father hated me because I had a motorbike and I was bringing his daughter down here. But as the years have gone by, and I look back on it, I can't really blame him. You are never going to stop men riding motorcycles and you are never going to stop girls that like riding on the back. In the summer there could be a couple of hundred bikes here — mainly British bikes. My motorcycle days were the best days of my life.'

Yvonne: 'We were sexless — we didn't — and no one went out with anybody. My dad said: "You be in at 11 o'clock." I would reply: "I can't, its all happening at 11 o'clock". And he said: "All those down and outs". It wasn't druggies and junkies because we never took anything. Then one day he said that he was coming up to look. He came up here and said: "They're nice. You're all right." And I was allowed to go there. We were here every single night, every weekend. We all went everywhere together.'

'Quite often I used to have young lads waiting for me on their bikes outside the DeMarco ice cream bar if I was going to the Ace to meet Ronald. They would try to race me there and on one occasion beat me. I was so upset that I threw my Tiger Cub against the wall and said: "It only does 75 m.p.h., I never want to ride it again!" Well, later that evening, on my way home, the boys were waiting for me again and wanted to race round the Iron Bridge. Ron, who had a Triumph Trophy at the time, would normally ride behind and leave me to it if I was racing anybody but he was not happy this time so decided to break it up. He came past like a dose of salts; we could not believe the speed he negotiated the bend that we all just slowed down and stopped in amazement. Ron could get round the bridge at a genuine 100 m.p.h. and I never knew anyone else who could do it as fast. Ron and I married in 1962. During our reception at The Pantiles, we both left to go down to the Ace while I was still in my wedding dress.

And in comes Jenny who we saw featured on the front page of *Today* (see page 85). 'I was 14 when I first rode a motorbike. I believe that I was one of the first girls to ride their own bike so I was always picked on by photographers visiting the Ace. At 16 I purchased a 199 c.c. Triumph Tiger Cub SL *(right)* which was the new trials version. I had the petrol tank sprayed blue because I hated having a small bike and it made it look like the Bonneville. It was a bit of a come-down as I had previously been riding a 650 c.c. but after 1960, if you had not passed your test, you could only ride a bike under 250 c.c. Ronald Wittich and Adrian Cooper (nick named 'Ace') had been going to the Ace cafe and the Busy Bee since 1957 and, in my opinion, were the fastest lads on two wheels. I had always admired Ron who was quite unassuming and never bragged about how well or fast he could ride, although we all knew that he was a man completely without fear. Ronald taught me how to ride properly, always with safety in mind and used to take me over to the rubbish dump across the road to teach me trials and scrambles.

'This is me on a borrowed Harley outside the Ace.'

Ron Wittich crashed while leading the Zandvoort Six Hour Endurance race on his Laverda and was taken unconscious to the local hospital. Although no bones were broken, Ron was heavily concussed and is likely to be detained for at least two weeks. His riding partner was Jan Strijbis.

Motor Cycle News, August 25, 1971

Ron Wittich, 32, a leading production racer and club rider, was killed at the Zandvoort six-hours production race in Holland on Saturday. He died instantly when he crashed his 750cc Laverda with 1½ hours of the race to run. At the time, he and his partner, Dutchman Jan Strijbis, were only a lap behind the leaders.

Only the previous weekend, Wittich was the best Briton in the Liege 24 hours production race in Belgium, when he and Doug Cash took a 750 Laverda to third place.

He lived in Luton, and was a married man with a family.

Motor Cycle News, August 30, 1972

'There have been some excellent times down here — really excellent. We used to race from here to the Busy Bee most nights, sometimes up to five abreast across the road, for something to do. We would also close the North Circular at either end for a Le Mans start. We would line all the bikes in the layby across the road and all stand on the wall. Somebody would shout: "Go!" and we would rush over . . . kick-start our bikes . . . and roar off. I was stopped one day on the North Circular for speeding. My hair was long so I used to keep it tucked under my helmet. The policeman who stopped me started swearing at me and saying that if I was killed he would have to tell my mother that I was splattered all over the road, and he took out his handkerchief and pretended to cry. He gave me a good telling off and said that I should know better. I tried to indicate that I was a female by fluttering my eyelashes and eventually took off my helmet. He looked at me in horror: "You're a woman!" he exclaimed. "What is the world coming to. Don't let me catch you again." As he got on his bike he winked at me: "Next time I would like to see you in a skirt!"'

'Ron progressed to production bike racing and doubled for Dudley Sutton in *The Leather Boys*. George Kent stood in for Colin Campbell and I doubled for Rita. This picture of Ron and me was taken in 1961 at Oulton Park when he had just come first on his Thruxton Triumph Bonneville in the Hector Dugdale Trophy race.'

And so for the Brighton burn-up — with a thousand screaming bikes! *Above and below left:* **First on the starting grid at 6.45 a.m. Duncan Shaw from Watford on his Triumph Speed Triple.** *Below right:* **As a nice contrast, the second man in — Dave Dixon from Chalfont St. Peter — came on his 40-year-old BSA A10.**

From then on, the bikes arrived fast and furious for what promised to be a beautiful summer run to the coast.

On Sunday, September 9, riders of all creeds went for a day at the seaside for the Ace Cafe Reunion at Brighton, Sussex. Madeira Drive on the seafront was not far short of being a miracle mile of motorcycles as thousands arrived from all over Europe.

Organiser Mark Wilsmore who had 'ten minutes' sleep that weekend said the turn-out was a record, claiming a total of 30,000 overall attended the weekend events in London and Brighton.

Classic Bike, November 2001

The safety car onto the North Circular was piloted by PC Steve Harnden with PC Rick Campbell on the radio — present day contemporaries to Tony Purbrick, Ron Jamieson and John Gillett — but now based at the new traffic police garage for the Wembley area at Alperton.

Hundreds of bikes joined the southbound lane, swamping startled motorists. But the speed was sedate, not like the old days . . . yet nothing changes as the North Circular still holds one of the worst accident records . . .

London's North Circular Road, orbiting the northern half of the capital, is home to two of the country's worst accident hotspots. At one, the junction between the A406 North Circular Road and the A109 Bounds Green Road, the Department for Transport, Local Government and the Regions estimates there will be 6,690 accidents over the next 30 years, leading to an annual toll of three deaths and 284 injured. Farther west, the A406's junction with the Golders Green Road will be responsible for 590 accidents over a 30-year period, the DTLR estimates.

To rectify these, the DTLR is proposing to spend £252.4 million building an underpass at the A109 junction. At the Golders Green Road junction, it has earmarked £35.3 million to improve safety.

The Daily Telegraph, November 10, 2001

. . . but does he realise that he has just passed Noddy's escape route, we ask?!

So let us give the last word to Noddy who so admirably set the scene for us as it was back in the Golden Years. One of Barry's adversaries then was PC Ron Jamieson, who finally nailed the young tearaway on January 15, 1961 (see page 100), so we persuaded them both to meet once more . . . on their old battleground . . . but under completely different circumstances!

Exactly 41 years later, on a cold blustery January morning, they stood together overlooking the Ace, alive with the sounds of bikes arriving and departing along the old 'Circular'. It was a moment neither of them could ever have envisaged in their wildest dreams . . . but then some dreams — like Mark Wilsmore's — do come true!

Ron became an instructor on the motorcycle wing of the Police Driving School at Hendon but later returned to normal traffic patrol duties. He was a member of the Special Escort Group providing motorcycle escorts for visiting Royalty and Heads of State. He retired from the force in 1974. Both his sons joined the service (CID, not Traffic); one having now retired and the other due within the next two years.

Barry settled down, married and had a son. He took a job at Hamrax Motors (of the dodgy number plates saga) in Ladbroke Grove as a mechanic on bikes and three-wheelers, and later moved on to Raybury Motors in Kilburn. He then joined London Underground, first as a guard and then as a driver before becoming a driver-instructor. He retired in 1999 and now devotes his life to caring for his elderly mum.